GLOBETROTTER™

VISITOR'S

TAMAN NEGARA

Malaysia's Premier National Park

DAVID BOWDEN

NH
NEW
HOLLAND

This edition published in 2001 by
New Holland Publishers (UK) Ltd
London • Cape Town • Sydney • Auckland

First published in 2000

Garfield House
86 Edgware Road
London W2 2EA
United Kingdom

80 McKenzie Street
Cape Town 8001
South Africa

14 Aquatic Drive
Frenchs Forest, NSW 2086
Australia

218 Lake Road
Northcote
Auckland
New Zealand

ISBN 1 85974 259 9

Publishing Manager: Jo Hemmings
Editor: Mike Unwin
Copy Editor: Philip Cheek
Artwork: Jan Wilczur (birds), Mike Unwin (all others)
Cartographer: Bill Smuts
Designer: Alan Marshall
Indexer: Janet Dudley
Production: Joan Woodroffe

Reproduction by Modern Age Repro House Limited, Hong Kong
Printed and bound in Malaysia by Times Offset (M) Sdn Bhd

Photographic Credits:
Andrew Bannister, pp. 18 (top), 59 (top): **David Bowden**, pp. 19 (top), 37 (top), 38 (bottom), 58 (top right), 77 (top right), 79 (bottom), 90 (bottom), 91 (bottom left), 110 (top, bottom); **Alain Compost**, pp. 57 (bottom), 59 (bottom), 78 (bottom), 90 (top), 109 (top), 111 (bottom); **Gerald Cubitt**, Cover, pp. 17, 18 (bottom), 19 (bottom), 20, 40, 57 (top), 58 (top left, bottom), 60 (top, bottom left, bottom right), 77 (bottom), 78 (top), 79 (top, centre left, centre right), 80, 91 (top, bottom right), 92 (top left, top right, bottom), 109 (centre, bottom), 112; **Malaysia Tourism Promotion**, pp. 39 (top), 77 (top left); **Raleigh International**, pp. 37 (bottom), 89 (top, bottom); **Arthur Teng**, pp 38 (top), 39 (bottom), 111 (top)

To my parents for opening my eyes to nature, and to Zoe and Maria Bowden - may their eyes always be open to nature.

Contents

Acknowledgements

This guidebook is the result of many pleasurable hours travelling through Taman Negara and many more compiling details on the park so that more people can appreciate its natural wonders.

Thanks go to my wife, Maria, for accompanying me on my fieldwork and for assisting with compiling the text, Ken Scriven for co-ordinating the book in Malaysia, and Jo Hemmings and Mike Unwin from New Holland Publishers for their editorial skills. The assistance of various officers from the Department of Wildlife and National Parks was very much appreciated. In particular, thanks go to the Director General, Musa bin Nordin for recognising the value of this guide and for co-ordinating his officers in the various sections of the park. Ahmad Shamsuddin, Director of the Terengganu State Wildlife and National Parks Department offered invaluable assistance for my fieldwork on Tasik Kenyir and the Terengganu side of the park. Jasmi bin Abdus, the Director, DWNPPN Perak State, provided meticulous editing of the section on the park's trails. Sabarudin bin Mat Kari, Deputy Wildlife Officer, provided information on the Merapoh access to the park.

I am indebted to Ken Rubeli for his assistance with the track notes throughout the Pahang side of the park.

Anthony Wong from Asian Overland Services provided excellent support and advice on the tourism elements of Taman Negara. Thanks also go to Masood M. Yusof from the Taman Negara Resort for his generous support and to guides Roslan Kassim and Safarin Mohd for their professionalism. Yassim helped open my eyes to the park's many natural attractions.

While these people helped, in the end I take full responsibility for the accuracy of the text.

David Bowden

About the author

David Bowden is a freelance writer based in Kuala Lumpur, Malaysia. David came from Australia to Malaysia over ten years ago to take up a position with the World Wide Fund for Nature (WWF) Malaysia and has since had the opportunity to travel extensively throughout the country.

Since finishing his contract with WWF, David has worked with UNESCO in Cambodia and has subsequently pursued a career in public relations and photojournalism. This has enabled him to travel to most of Malaysia's wildlife centres and parks, including Taman Negara on many occasions.

David has written guides to Cambodia, Thailand, Kuala Lumpur, the leading natural attractions of Malaysia, and more recently, has completed a teaching guide for the Mekong River.

Introducing Taman Negara, or National

Park, is one of the finest and oldest accessible rainforests in the world. Centrally located in a remote region of Peninsular Malaysia, it offers adventurous travellers an unparalleled opportunity to explore the rich natural wonders of unspoilt rainforest. Much of the park remains as it has been for the past 130 million

Taman

years or so. Originally set aside as a wildlife reserve in 1925 to protect game species, the park was established in 1939. Today at 4,343 square kilometres (1,676 square miles) it is the largest park on Peninsular Malaysia. Situated in the Tahan Range, it also includes the Peninsula's highest peak, Gunung Tahan at

Negara

2,187 metres (7,173 feet). As the park covers parts of three states, there are several main access routes. The most visited part is at Kuala Tahan in Pahang State and much of this guide refers to this area. The other, less-developed access points are also described here in detail.

Within the park there is a range of accommodation experiences available, ranging from true wilderness to comfortable resort-style facilities adjacent to the Park HQ at Kuala Tahan. Most visitors stay in the park for two to four days, though there are sufficient activities to keep adventurous visitors occupied for several weeks.

The riverboat journey to Kuala Tahan is, for some, as exciting as the rainforest itself. The introduction of a jetboat service now offers a thrilling alternative journey into and out from the park. Boats are an essential transportation element as there are no roads within the park.

Taman Negara has a variety of attractions to see and experience. The park is home to the original inhabitants of the area, the Orang Asli people, some of whom still follow a traditional semi-nomadic lifestyle of farming, fishing and hunting. They are the only people allowed to hunt and forage for food in the park.

The flora and fauna species list for Peninsular Malaysia is impressive, with an estimated 10,000 plants, 150,000 insects, 25,000 invertebrates, 675 birds, 270 reptiles, 250 freshwater fish and 200 mammals. Even today new species are being discovered. Undoubtedly there are more astonishing and important secrets locked up in this precious ecosystem just waiting to be revealed.

Many of Malaysia's species can be found in Taman Negara but visitors need to recognise that the park is large and the wildlife is often shy and well camouflaged. Visitors should appreciate that one of the main functions of national parks is to provide an undisturbed habitat for plants and animals. Should they be lucky enough to see any native creatures, this should be regarded as a privilege and a bonus. Go with the expectation that animals are difficult to see and that your chances of such sightings are remote. Improve your chances by taking binoculars, and if you have the luxury of an extended visit, spend some time in an isolated hide and let the animals come to you.

A trip to Taman Negara can be as relaxed or as energetic as you like. The facilities in the park provide for the varied needs of visitors, from those craving solitude to those chasing adventure.

There are limestone caves to explore, relaxing riverside fishing, shooting whitewater rapids, floating down

Rhinoceros Hornbill

peaceful rivers on tyre tubes, adventur- ous night-time safaris, birdwatching, investigating the forest canopy via a sus- pended walkway high above the rainfor- est floor, and guided walks to isolated parts of the park where few people have ever ventured.

> ## Purpose of the Park
>
> The stated purpose of the park is to utilise the land within the park in perpetuity, for the propagation, protection and preservation of the indigenous flora and fauna.

Enjoy Taman Negara, as there are few rainforest experiences in the world quite like it, and leave the park as you found it so that future generations of travellers will be able to share your appreciation of its many natural wonders.

The Park

The park, established in 1939, was once known as King George V Park. After Malaysia achieved independence it was renamed Taman Negara. The plants and animals have inhabited the area since long before this and indeed the rainforests here are considered some of the world's oldest. They have evolved over 100 million years.

The first section of the park originated from Pahang State Legislation in 1925 when over 1,300 square kilometres (500 square miles) of natural tropical rainforest were gazetted as the Gunung Tahan Game Reserve. Today, it covers an area of 434,350 hectares (over a million acres) in the states of Pahang, Terengganu and Kelantan. It is the most extensive protected area of pristine, lowland, evergreen rainforest in the country, where no commercial logging has occurred.

The Forest Experience

Taman Negara offers a variety of activities in a tropical rainforest setting. For many visitors, the sheer overwhelming thrill of the towering forest alone justifies a visit.

Approximately one third of all the world's flowering plants are found in Malaysia. The richness and diversity of species is partly due to the climatic conditions, combining high moisture and temperature. The largest plant community in Taman Negara is the lowland rainforest – where trees are the dominant life form, coexisting with shrubs, epiphytes, parasites, climbers, stranglers and saprophytes as well as small non-vascular plants such as lichens, bryophytes and fungi.

The rainforests of Malaysia start at sea level and are found up to altitudes of 1,200 metres (4,000 feet), where the lower montane forests take over to altitudes of 1,800 metres (6,000 feet).

To the first time visitor, Taman Negara may appear somewhat threatening, with its supposedly dangerous animals, impenetrable 'jungle', oppressive climate and isolation. There are many myths about the rainforest perpetuated through fiction down the ages. Many visitors to Taman Negara are pleasantly surprised by just how accessible and friendly the park feels once they are there.

The facilities at Kuala Tahan (site of the Park HQ) are very good and any idea that visitors will be really roughing it is quickly dispelled once they arrive. However, for the adventurous traveller, it is very easy to obtain a wilderness experience. Reaching these more isolated destinations is not a major problem as there is a very good river transport system and all trails to the main attractions are well maintained and clearly signposted.

Visitors soon learn that the really impenetrable forest only occurs around the riverbanks where there is a high incidence of direct sunlight. Within the rainforest, the dense canopy prevents much of the sunlight reaching the forest floor, and as a result, the plant life is not as prolific.

While there are many animals in the rainforest, most will remain unseen since they are shy and normally wary of the slightest human presence. Using the services of a guide will not only ensure safety but also improve the chances of seeing the unique features of the park, including, perhaps, some of its more elusive animals.

How To Use This Book

The *Globetrotter's Visitor's Guide to Taman Negara* is an exciting addition to the general travel guides to Malaysia. While some general travel information on Malaysia is available in this guide, it concentrates more on providing detailed information on the park and the range of adventure activities available in Taman Negara.

This guide is just that, a guide. While every effort has been made to document accurately the park and its activities for visitors, readers should be aware that there are very few things in this world that remain constant. Taman Negara is a dynamic rainforest ecosystem that is changing daily. While the changes in this natural system are slow compared to the rapid economic development of Malaysia's capital, Kuala Lumpur, they are, however, still evident.

This guide should be read thoroughly before setting out for Malaysia, since it provides all the essential information the visitor needs in order to plan and make the most of a trip to Taman Negara (see *Planning and Practicalities*, page 11). When in the park, this book is an invaluable guide to the many activities that can be enjoyed there (see *Activities and Adventure*, page 41). Taman Negara spreads over three Peninsular Malaysian states, and while most activities relate to the main Pahang entry to the park and principally those around Park HQ at Kuala Tahan, there is also mention of the less visited areas in Terengganu, Kelantan and Merapoh, where relevant.

The information on plant and animal (see *Life in the Forest*, page 49) provides a general introduction to many of the species that the visitor may encounter. However it should not be regarded as an exhaustive account. For the more serious enthusiast, there are several useful field guides to help you identify the wildlife of the region (see *Further Reading*, page 123), that should be used in conjunction with this guide. For birdwatchers, this guide provides the first full checklist of all bird species recorded in the park (see page 124).

This guide has adopted international timing based upon a 24-hour clock so that eight o'clock in the morning is referred to as 0800 and eight in the evening is 2000.

The Glossary on page 126 gives simple definitions of a number of technical and scientific terms that occur in the text, whilst all abbreviations used in the book are explained opposite.

Abbreviations

AC	Air conditioned
a.s.l.	Above sea level
DANCED	Danish Co-operation for Environment and Development
DWNPPN	Department of Wildlife and National Parks of Peninsular Malaysia
FRIM	Forest Research Institute of Malaysia
GMT	Greenwich Mean Time
HQ	Headquarters
KL	Kuala Lumpur
KLIA	Kuala Lumpur International Airport
MAS	Malaysian Airlines
MNS	Malaysian Nature Society
MTPB	Malaysian Tourism Promotion Board
NGO	Non Governmental Organisation
Perhilitan	Department of Wildlife and National Parks of Peninsular Malaysia
PJ	Petaling Jaya, the main suburb of Kuala Lumpur
RM	Ringgit Malaysian, the currency in Malaysia divisible by 100 sen
TNR	Taman Negara Resort
WWF	World Wide Fund for Nature

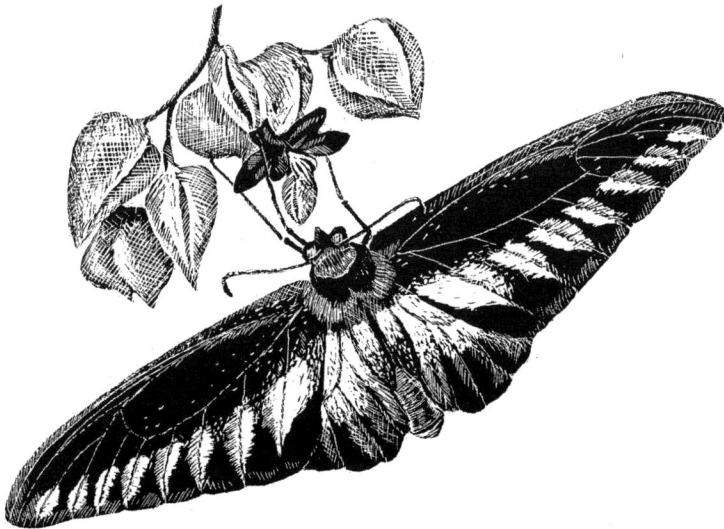

LOCATION: Spread over areas of Pahang, Kelantan and Terengganu; 59 km (37 miles) upriver from Kuala Tembeling, which is 54 km (34 miles) north of Temerloh on the Kuala Lumpur-to-Kuantan road.

CLIMATE: 25°–37°C (77°–99°F). Typically hot and humid, but cool and sunny in the mountains and cold on peaks at night. More rain expected October–February.

WHEN TO GO: The best time to visit Taman Negara is from March to September, when the climate is drier and generally more favourable for walking and watching wildlife. Visitors to the park at other times should expect heaver rainfall and the wettest period is between November and mid January, which can restrict movements in some parts of the park.

ACCESS: Jerantut is the main entry point to Taman Negara and is a three hour drive away from Kuala Lumpur. Alternatively take a taxi or train to Kuala Tembeling on the Singapore-to-Kota Bharu line. You can also take a boat trip from the Taman Negara jetty at Kuala Tembeling, up the Sungai Tembeling, to the Park HQ at Kuala Tahan. There are alternative access points in Kelantan and Terengganu.

PERMITS: Bookings for park boats and accommodation are made with agents such as Taman Negara Resort office in Kuala Lumpur, but shop around for other operators or ask at Kuala Tahan. Entry, camera and fishing fees are payable at the Park HQ at Kuala Tahan.

EQUIPMENT: Hiking, camping and fishing equipment is available for hire in the park. Remember to take a reliable torch for night walks. Light trousers, leech socks and training shoes should be worn in the forest, with warmer clothing if you are intending to climb. Walking boots and sleeping bags, insect repellent and a plastic water bottle are essential for serious hiking.

FACILITIES: The Pahang entrance to the park has a reception and information centre, chalets, camping area, restaurants - the Tahan Restaurant and the Teresek Cafeteria, both serving Malaysian and international cuisine, a cocktail lounge and a shop, offering both souvenirs and provisions. There are also three visitors' lodges, two fishing lodges and six observation hides.

WATCHING WILDLIFE: There is excellent birdwatching throughout the park, with over 275 species recorded, and a wealth of reptiles, insects and plant life. Bats and snakes are found in the caves. Mammals such as wild pigs, deer, and tapir may be observed from the hides, while monkeys can be seen in the forest and otters along the rivers. Elusive mammals such as elephants, seladang (wild oxen), tigers, leopards and sun bears are seldom seen, although the visitor may find tracks and other signs of their presence. A variety of nocturnal creatures may be encountered on night excursions.

VISITOR ACTIVITIES: Walking and trekking, river trips, shooting the rapids, cave exploration, swimming, fishing, mountain climbing and watching birds and other wildlife.

Planning

Malaysia is one of the easiest Asian countries for the overseas traveller to visit. It has a well-developed infrastructure and a stable economic and political climate. Destinations are well signposted and English is widely understood

and

with most people in the country being either bi or trilingual.

The currency, the Ringgit, is based on units of ten and one hundred, making calculations easy. Measurements (distance, weight etc) are metric – kilometre and kilogram for example. The climate is hot and humid at all times of the year, with high rainfall.

Practicalities

There is a range of accommodation to suit every pocket, and visitors will find warmth and hospitality wherever they go. Malaysia is a multicultural country with Malay, Chinese, Indian, Orang Asli and a variety of smaller ethnic groups living in harmony. This rich cultural diversity results in an spectacular variety of foods, dance and festivals.

Getting To Malaysia

By Plane

Most overseas visitors will arrive in Malaysia by plane, though there are various other methods (see below).

Kuala Lumpur International Airport

The new RM 9 billion Kuala Lumpur International Airport (KLIA) at Sepang is an ultra-modern and welcoming sight after a long flight.

The arrivals procedure is straightforward and signs (in Bahasa Malaysia and English) are self-explanatory.

Major airlines

There are about 36 international carriers servicing the airport. Some of these, and their Kuala Lumpur phone numbers include:

Malaysian Airlines (MAS) (7463000)
Singapore Airlines (26982033)
Thai Airways (2012900)
Qantas/British Airways (21676188)
Cathay Pacific (2383355)
Lauda Air (2488033)
Northwest Airlines (21615130).

There are several modes of transport from KLIA to the city centre, 60 kilometres (37 miles) away. Prepaid coupons for budget and luxury taxis to the city are sold. Enquiries and bookings can be directed to Tel: 92238080. Normal city taxis can take passengers to KLIA and can now pick up from the airport using the meter. On these taxis, airport surcharges and tolls are paid by the passenger. The journey normally takes about one hour, depending upon the time of day and traffic conditions.

Frequent airport buses also operate to and from the city from 0645 to 0030. The city terminal is at Jalan Duta (Tel: 62033154). A high-speed rail connection is also planned from KL Sentral to KLIA.

Domestic Flights

Domestic flights operate from KLIA or from terminal 3 of the the former Subang International Airport (the latter will close once KLIA is accessible by high-speed rail). Getting to Taman Negara is similar from both airports.

While it is possible to fly to certain domestic airports to reach the various parts of Taman Negara, most visitors travel overland from KLIA or the city. The domestic airports that can be used are Kuantan and Kuala Terengganu, with several daily services from KLIA and Subang on MAS to both these destinations.

There are departure taxes of RM5 and RM40 for domestic and international flights respectively. In most cases this has been incorporated into the ticket price but travellers should check their tickets and have money available to save any embarrassment at the airport.

By Sea

These days, few visitors to Malaysia arrive by ship although it is possible through ports like Port Klang (the port for Kuala Lumpur), Penang and Langkawi. There are adequate transport links from these points to Taman Negara.

By Train

There are several main overland access points for road or rail travellers from Thailand to the north of Malaysia and the island-state of Singapore to the south. The train is popular for many budget conscious travellers passing through Asia. There is at least one daily service from both the north and south into Malaysia.

There are two train entry points from Thailand; Padang Besar on the west coast and Golok/Rantau Panjang on the east coast. Kuala Lumpur is the best place to alight from trains from Padang Besar for Taman Negara although it is possible to continue to Gemas and catch the Singapore to Kota Bharu train (the station for Kota Bharu is called Wakaf Bharu). For those who enter from Golok/Rantau Panjang, it is necessary to catch a taxi or bus from the Thai border to Pasir Mas to connect to the Kota Bharu to Singapore train.

The Kota Bharu to Singapore service is the best connection to Taman Negara for those entering the park from Southeast Thailand.

For more details on train travel contact Tel: 22738000.

Immigration, Visas and Customs

All visitors to Malaysia require a valid passport and must complete a Disembarkation Card, which is printed in English. Most visitors are granted a two month visa-free stay upon arrival, however, this is best confirmed by the nearest Malaysian Embassy prior to travel to Malaysia.

Once in the country, visa extensions may be sought from the nearest Immigration Office, especially the headquarters in Kuala Lumpur (Tel : 255 5077). Certain items (e.g. taped videos) need to be declared on the Customs Declaration Form and presented to Customs officers before leaving the airport. A Traveller's Declaration Form (see **Currency** page 15) must also be completed to declare all Malaysian and foreign currency. All plant derivatives must be declared to the Plant Quarantine Office.

Drugs are taken very seriously by the Malaysian authorities, and those convicted of drug trafficking can face the death penalty.

Local Time

All of Malaysia shares a single time zone. This is 8 hours ahead of GMT all year round.

Electricity

Electricity is available in all but the most isolated villages in Malaysia. The system is 240-volt 50-cycle. For equipment that operates on a different system, adapters are available, though if in doubt it is best to bring your own. In Taman Negara, a generator supplies electricity around the clock at Kuala Tahan and during the early evening in the more remote camps, so lighting and cooling is available when most needed.

Health Regulations

Travellers entering Malaysia do not require cholera vaccinations, but for those entering from certain areas like Africa and South America, vaccination against Yellow Fever may be required. If in doubt, consult your doctor or travel agent.

General Health

For something as important as health, travellers should consult their doctor rather than depend upon this guide. Prevention is always better than cure and while the point of visiting Taman Negara is to discover the wonders of nature, a few useful tips should ensure a more enjoyable holiday.

Medical facilities in the country are good; however, Taman Negara is an isolated destination that is some distance from specialist help. Basic medical assistance is provided by the local clinic. The climate is very hot and humid and visitors need to maintain body fluids and salt levels. As a precaution, avoid strenuous activity in the heat of the day, wear a hat, sunglasses, sunscreen, appropriate clothing (both for the climate and cultural sensitivities) and drink lots of water.

Malaysia is a malaria and dengue fever area (though Taman Negara is basically malaria-free) and a physician should be consulted regarding one of several prophylaxis on the market. Both these diseases are carried by mosquitoes, and although incidence is low, both are potentially fatal. It is therefore best to take precautions against being bitten. Mosquitoes are most active at dusk and dawn, so during these times, where possible, stay in screened areas. Use an insect repellent and wear light coloured clothing with long sleeves and long trousers.

While food preparation in the country is mostly hygienic, the spiciness of Malaysian food may present some problems to first time travellers. A good principle is *boil it, cook it, peel it or leave it, if* you are concerned about your food. Others would disagree and argue that if you are this careful you will miss out on the many delights of Malaysian food. As a rule, be careful, but not to the extent of letting worry overshadow your holiday. While the water quality in the country is high, various bottled waters are available for the more cautious.

Despite the array of exotic tropical diseases, the most likely medical problem is traveller's diarrhoea as stomachs adjust to new dietary regimes. This is mostly due to *Escherichia coli (E. coli),* a common bacterium present in different strains in most countries. Should you be unlucky enough to be afflicted, it will most likely only last a few days and cause some discomfort. As a rule, solid foods should be avoided, fluids main-

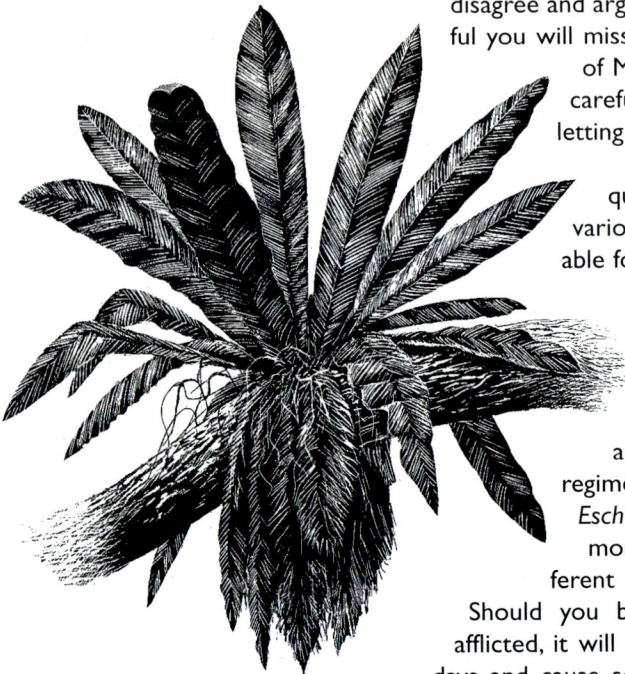

Bird's-nest Fern

tained and rehydration salts consumed. Basically, your body is trying to rid itself of the germs and as a natural bodily function it should be allowed to take its course. Severe and prolonged diarrhoea requires medical attention.

It is worth packing a small first aid kit, especially for isolated areas like Taman Negara. Useful items include rehydration salts (diarrhoea), *Loperamide* or *Immodium* (diarrhoea), insect repellent, eye drops, antiseptic lotion, antifungal powder, a general antibiotic and plaster. Women's sanitary products are readily available but worth packing just in case.

Staying Cool

A few simple tips can help first-time visitors to Malaysia to cope with the tropical heat and humidity:

• Take regular, tepid showers
• Drink large amounts of water
• Use salt on food
• Wear a shady hat
• Use high-factor suncream
• Wear loose clothing made of natural fibres

Currency and Credit Cards

The Malaysian currency is known as the Ringgit (RM) and there are 100 sen to each Ringgit. Notes come in denominations of: RM 1, RM 2, RM 5, RM 10, RM 20, RM 50 and RM 100. Denominations of RM 500 and RM 1000 were once in circulation but are no longer legal tender in Malaysia. There are coins of the following denominations: 1, 5, 10, 20, 50 sen and RM 1.

Asian exchange rates have varied greatly over the past few years and the following should be used as a guide only – RM 3.8 to 1 $US, RM 5.5 to 1 Pound Sterling, RM 2 to 1$ Aust..

There are moneychangers and banks with currency exchanges throughout the country. Recent currency controls restrict the flow of currency into and out of the country. Foreigners and non-residents are allowed to carry not more than RM1,000 and an unlimited amount of foreign currency when entering or leaving the country. However, the amount declared upon departure cannot exceed that declared when entering the country.

Major credit cards (Visa, Mastercard, Diners and Amex) and travellers' cheques are accepted, including at the Taman Negara Resort.

Tipping is not essential, though in big establishments a 10% service charge may be incorporated into the final bill. However, small change is normally left and those who offer exceptional service are usually rewarded.

Customs, Etiquette and Dress

Malaysia is a multicultural country. Its 21 million people comprise Malay, Chinese, Indian and various indigenous communities.

Malaysia is also an Islamic state, with approximately 60% of the population practising this religion. Many Malaysian people dress conservatively and are often offended by those who dress more liberally. Excessive exposure is therefore considered inappropriate and bathers who swim in the rivers of Taman Negara should wear sensible swimming costumes. Nude swimming or sunbathing is offensive to many Malaysians. Outward signs of physical affection between people of the opposite sex are normally frowned upon.

There are various acceptable codes of behaviour in visiting a mosque or *surau* (Moslem prayer room) and one should consult a Moslem friend before entering various parts of mosques. For example, shoes are not worn inside a mosque and many other Malaysian buildings. A collection of shoes near the door will indicate whether one should remove one's shoes.

Clothing should be functional, practical and culturally sensitive. The dress code in Taman Negara is casual, with few opportunities to dress up even at the Taman Negara Resort. Light clothing, in both weight and colour, is recommended. Natural cotton is preferable to synthetics as it breathes more easily. A raincape is essential to stay dry in the forest.

Language

The official language is Bahasa Malaysia, although many Malaysians speak several languages and will use them all in general conversation. A similar language is spoken in southern Thailand, Indonesia, Brunei and parts of the island of Mindanao in the Philippines. Several Chinese dialects and Tamil are also spoken widely throughout Malaysia.

English is widely understood, especially in the cities and by tour operators and guides in Taman Negara. Many words have been adapted from English, so English speaking tourists will notice many words they can understand. There is usually someone around who can help out in translating.

Forest Language

air panas (hot spring)
air terjun (waterfall)
bandar (town)
batang (main river)
batu (stone)
besar (big)
bukit (hill)
bumbun (hide)
gua (cave)
gunung (mountain)
hitam (black)
hutan simpan (forest reserve)
hutan rekreasi/hutan lipur (recreational forest)
jalan (road)
jeram (rapids)
jenut (salt lick)
kampung (village)
kecil (small)
khemah (camp)
kuala (river mouth)
lata (cascade)

lubuk (deep pool)
mat salleh (general term for foreigner)
negara (national)
padang (field)
pantai (beach)
pengkalan (jetty)
pondok (hut/shelter)
pulau (island)
puteh (white)
rentis (jungle trail)
simpang (junction)
sungai (river)
taman (park)
tasik (lake)
tanjung (cape)
teluk (bay)
ulu (upper reaches of a river).

one (*satu*), two (*dua*), three (*tiga*), four(*empat*), five (*lima*), six (*enam*), seven (*tujuh*), eight (*lapan*), nine (*sembilan*) and ten (*sepuluh*).

UNSPOILT RAINFOREST OVER 130 MILLION YEARS OLD CARPETS THE ROLLING HILLS OF TAMAN NEGARA.

ABOVE: FACILITIES AT THE PARK ARE MANAGED BY THE TAMAN NEGARA RESORT WHICH PROVIDES A VARIETY OF ROOMS, FROM SUPERIOR CHALETS TO BASIC HOSTELS.

LEFT: IN THE NORTH OF THE PARK, KUALA KENIAM CAMP IS SITUATED DEEP IN THE FOREST AND OFFERS A QUIETER RETREAT FOR THOSE SEEKING SOLITUDE AND TRANQUILITY.

OPPOSITE ABOVE: WOODEN SAMPANS PROVIDE TRANSPORT INTO THE PARK AND BETWEEN CAMPS ALONG THE TEMBELING RIVER.

OPPOSITE BELOW: ACCOMMODATION IS AVAILABLE IN HIDES FOR THOSE WHO WISH TO STAY OVERNIGHT AND OBSERVE THE ANIMALS.

A BOAT TRIP UP RIVER TAKES VISITORS BENEATH A GALLERY OF HUGE OVERHANGING DIPTEROCARP TREES.

Many Bahasa Malaysia names of places, rivers, mountains and towns are used throughout this guide. A little knowledge of the language will enhance any visit to Malaysia and Taman Negara.

Climate
The country is located within 150 kilometres (95 miles) north of the Equator (Latitudes 2 – 7 degrees North), and the climate is best described as tropical with a uniformly high temperature. This means it is hot and humid with a high rainfall all year round, especially in the lowlands. Taman Negara is no different except at the higher altitudes of Gunung Tahan where temperatures can drop to freezing. For first time visitors the weather can be oppressive, especially the constantly high humidity, so avoid the heat of the day and drink lots of water to avoid dehydration. The dense vegetation of the rainforest modifies the effects of sunlight but in exposed areas, like the main river, the effects of the sun can be intense. While boating on the river, the passing draught of breeze may disguise the burning effects of the sun, so be cautious.

The evenings are pleasant and rain showers bring relief. Rainfall is common (after all it is a *rain*forest), although it rarely lasts for long periods, with frequent rainstorms in the afternoon and evening. These storms are monsoonal, i.e. there is seasonal variation in winds caused by alternating high and low pressure cells over Central Asia. In general, the east coast of Malaysia is affected by the monsoonal rains from October to March and the west coast from September through December. Inland, the monsoonal effects are not as marked, although the wettest period is mid November to mid January when localised flooding could restrict movement within some parts of the park. A marker near the top of the arrival steps at the TNR indicates the height of the 1971 flood. Campers also need to realise that many small streams rise suddenly after rain, so should not camp too near the banks.

The driest month for Kuala Tahan is February with seven centimetres (2 inches), and the wettest October with 27 centimetres (10 inches). Annual rainfall is about 220 centimetres (85 inches) in the lowlands and nearly 400 centimetres (160 inches) in the mountainous regions.

Communications
Malaysia is well connected to terrestrial, satellite and electronic communications networks. Public phones accept coins or a variety of phonecards purchased from stores that display the sign *Kadfon*. Local, domestic and international telephone calls may be made from some but not all settlements in Taman Negara – for example there is telephone access in the Kuala Tahan area but not in Terengganu or Kuala Koh. There are no phones in the rooms of the Taman Negara Resort but there are public phones that accept both coins and phonecards (sold in the resort mini-mart).

Safety
Malaysia is a relatively safe country to travel through, with few physical threats. Most of the reported crime appears to be petty, with robberies and snatchings about all a visitor may encounter. Travellers should take the usual precautions such as keeping

separate records of travel documents, traveller's cheques and credit cards. A con-cealed money pouch is advisable but not essential. Visitors should take care in areas where pickpockets operate, such as crowded bus stations, shopping malls and mar-kets. The Taman Negara Resort has safe deposit boxes at the front office.

Travel insurance is always wise in case of theft, illness or other problems. The cost and degree of cover can vary greatly so it is advisable to shop around for the best policy – for example expensive items like cameras may have limited cover.

Women Travelling Alone

Most women should not be threatened by travelling alone or with others in Malaysia. Some Malaysians may ask whether single women are married or attached – more out of curiosity than anything. It is probably best to dismiss enquiries with a friendly smile. Single women should take the same safety measures as other travellers (see *Safety* page 21).

Travelling With Children

Travelling with children always has its own special complications, but travel in Malaysia and to Taman Negara is not that difficult. Parents need to be aware that Taman Negara is an isolated location with limited medical facilities and evacuation procedures. The park has been established so that visitors can observe a tropical rainforest, something that may not be high in the minds of many travelling children. While there are many animals living in the rainforest, observing them is very much a matter of luck and patience, and most young children will not be capable of sitting quiet and still in a jun-gle hide for hours for the possible sighting of a feeding animal at dusk. The park has facilities for children's recreation and the trails around Park HQ in Kuala Tahan are well maintained and negotiable by most visitors. However, a backpack baby carrier is a better idea than a stroller (buggy). It is best to avoid the heat of the day for young children.

The Mousedeer Trail at Kuala Tahan has been designed with children in mind and trained guides lead nature discovery walks. Staff can also organise art activities, nature games and viewings of nature videos.

Shopping

Throughout the large cities of Malaysia, shops are open daily from 1000 – 2200. Markets, especially food markets, are popular in the early morning and late evening as many Malaysians like to buy fresh ingredients for cooking. *Pasar malam* or night-mar-kets are popular and locations vary daily, so if you are in a large city ask a local for the nearest.

In some places, bargaining may be acceptable and in others, the prices are fixed. If you are unsure, politely make a reasonable offer to determine the response of the sales staff. As a rule, prices for goods sold in street markets and small stores are negotiable but the prices are fixed in large department stores. Most prices in and around Taman Negara are fixed, but you can always try your luck, especially for bulk purchases.

Getting to Taman Negara

Taman Negara can be reached via three main park entrances. Of these, the most important - and the standard route for most travellers - is via Kuala Tahan. The journey to Kuala Tahan is an exciting one requiring a road or rail as well as a river journey. Access to the other main parts of the park are adequate but public transport is not that well developed.

Kuala Tahan, Pahang

By Air
Flying is not really an option to the main part of the park as KLIA is the most accessible airport. While Kuantan Airport may be the closest it is not advisable to use this as the overland connections from KLIA to the park are better.

By Road and River
Most visitors to Taman Negara will commence their journey from Kuala Lumpur – for them the main park access is via the Sungai Tembeling in Pahang. The departure point is from Kuala Tembeling near Jerantut, 230 kilometres (140 miles) or about three to four hours drive from Kuala Lumpur and 220 kilometres (135 miles) or two and a half hours from Kuantan.

From here it is a two to three hour journey by sampan, depending on water levels, to travel the 69 kilometres (43 miles) to the Park HQ at Kuala Tahan. Alternatively, there is a 75 kilometre (46 mile) – two hours – rough road journey from Jerantut to Park HQ.

There are several ways to get to Kuala Tembeling either via private or public transport. Private or rental cars are the most convenient and fastest, and secure parking is available near the jetty wharf for a daily parking fee.

Buses and long distance taxis regularly travel to the park from the Pudu Raya Bus Station in Kuala Lumpur (Tel: 2300145) or the main bus terminus in Kuantan. Taman Negara Resort can arrange return transfers from the Hotel Istana in Kuala Lumpur to the resort for a

Crested Fireback Pheasant

fee. Daily departure time from the Istana is 0800.

For independent travellers the last 16 kilometres (10 miles) from Jerantut to Kuala Tembeling ferry wharf is a bus or taxi ride (Tel : 09 2664537). A new river terminal offers good facilities. Here visitors can choose between fast or regular boats to the park.

Jetboat Schedule

Depart Kuala Tahan	Arrive Kuala Tembeling
1000	1045
Depart Kuala Tembeling	Arrive Kuala Tahan
1300	1345

Regular, slim wooden sampan boats equipped with life vests depart from Kuala Tembeling at intervals from between 0900 to 1400 (up to 1430 on Fridays). Each boat carries about 10 passengers and the motors tend to be noisy. In the opposite direction boats depart from the early morning.

The Taman Negara Resort has recently acquired two New Zealand built jetboats that can reach the Park HQ in just 45 minutes as opposed to the two to three hours by slower boats. These 12-seater jetboats offer a thrilling, but more expensive ride and visitors may want to go one way on the jetboat and the other via the slower boat to experience both. Pregnant women and children under 10 years old use the jetboat at their own risk.

By River

The wharf at Kuala Tembeling for departures to Taman Negara is situated on the Jelai River near the junction with the Sungai Tembeling. Just below this junction, the river becomes the Sungai River. At 300 kilometres (190 miles), the Sungai Pahang is the longest in Peninsular Malaysia.

At the 35 kilometres (22 mile) mark of the journey signposts near Kuala Atok announce the beginning of Taman Negara. The undisturbed national park riverbank is in marked contrast to the other bank which has been partially cleared for agriculture and village settlements.

Most visitors arriving by riverboat tend to sleep their way to the park, probably as a result of their long journey from Kuala Lumpur. This is not to suggest there are not things to see along the way.

Wildlife tends to be rather sparse, due mainly to the continuous flow of somewhat noisy boats passing by. The speed at which the boats travel does not aid serious wildlife spotting. Moving branches may indicate monkey activity, so have a closer look. Some waterbirds are evident, especially the bright azure coloured kingfishers that dart close to the water's edge and occasionally stop to rest on an overhanging branch. Between April and July look for the large colonial nest sites of Blue-throated Bee-eaters in the cliff faces adjoining the river, and their low-level swooping flight as they hunt for insects over the river. Birds of prey such as fish eagles may also be seen perched on branches overlooking the river searching for prey. Hornbills may be spotted gliding over the river in search of fruiting trees.

By Road

There is an overland route from Jerantut to Park HQ. The road is mostly unsealed and a little rough and therefore appeals more to 4 x 4 enthusiasts. A daily minibus service operated by Ismail Travel and Tours leaves Kuala Tahan for Jerantut at 0800. The two-hour, 70 kilometre (43 mile) journey passes through plantations and small rural villages. Contact Tel : 09 2669109 for details.

By Rail

The nearest railway station to park HQ is Jerantut on the Singapore/Johor Bahru to Kota Bharu (Tumput) line. There are several trains a day from Kuala Lumpur to Gemas where you change to the Singapore to Tumput train.

From Jerantut, proceed to Kuala Tembeling by bus or taxi and then by boat to Taman Negara.

The main problem with train travel is that the connections are not very good and travellers have to wait for extended periods to enter the park. The one train from Kuala Lumpur leaves daily at 2020 and arrives at Jerantut at 0148 the next morning. The return train to Kuala Lumpur departs at 2355 and arrives at 0630 the next morning. The international train from Singapore arrives at 0329. There are three classes on the trains: first and second class offer sleepers, while third class is seating only

For further train information contact KTM Berhad (Malaysian Railway), Tel: 22738000, e-mail: passenger@ktmb.com.my.

Kuala Koh, Kelantan

Kuala Koh is a difficult part of the park to access, especially for international visitors. Public transport to the park (apart from taxis) is non-existent and few travel operators have organised itineraries. This entrance to the park is more suited to visitors with their own transport, preferably a 4 x 4 vehicle. The preferred mode of transport for independent visitors is to catch a bus or train to Gua Musang from Kuala Lumpur. From here hire a taxi all the way to the park and arrange for the taxi to return on a designated day for the return journey.

By Air

While Kota Bharu is the nearest airport, KLIA is still the more accessible for most visitors (see page 12).

By Road

Park HQ is 289 kilometres (179 miles) from Kuala Lumpur and 185 kilometres (115 miles) by road from Kota Bharu for visitors coming from the east coast. The nearest town is Gua Musang some 80 kilometres (50 miles) away. The journey from Gua Musang takes about 90 minutes and is best done in a 4 x 4 vehicle as the last 15 kilometres (9 miles) to the park is unsealed (caution must be exercised on these roads that service the plantations along the way). While the park entrance is well signposted at the Aring Junction on the Gua Musang to Kota Bharu Road, the remaining 45 kilometres (28 miles) is not well signposted. Taxis in Gua Musang may take visitors to the park although many are reluctant due to the condition of the road. Don't forget to organise a date to be collected. Catching a bus to the Aring Junction is not advisable as there are seldom taxis here to complete the last part of the journey.

By Rail
Daily trains from Singapore and Gemas arrive in Gua Musang. Details are best obtained first from Tel: 2273 8000.

Overland
The 16-day walk from Kuala Tahan at Taman Negara Park HQ to Kuala Koh should only be attempted by the fit and experienced, with guides and adequate equipment.

Terengganu
There are several ways of reaching the Terengganu side of the park, with a vehicle being the preferred mode. Flying or catching a bus to Kuala Terengganu is an option for independent travellers. From here, taxis will deliver you directly to Pengkalan Gawi, Tasik Kenyir (Lake Kenyir) and ultimately, the park entrance. From the park entrance, the journey is by water to the far southern sections of this massive dammed lake. The actual Park Ranger Station located at Tanjung Mentong is a 90-minute fast boat journey from Pengkalan Gawi. Tasik Kenyir is one of the country's major nature-based tourism attractions and should not be overlooked.

By Air
Visitors can fly domestically to Kuala Terengganu on MAS from KLIA and on MAS or Pelangi Air from Terminal 3 at Subang Airport (the domestic terminal of the former international airport).

By Road and Water
There are several roads leading to Tasik Kenyir, 55 kilometres (34 miles) from Kuala Terengganu. The major turn off is at Ajil for Kuala Berang. Both these settlements are accessible from Kuala Terengganu to the north and Dungun to the south. The lake gateway at Pengkalan Gawi is well signposted with the last turn towards the lake at Kampong Kuala Jeneris. The road journey from Kuala Terengganu takes about one hour. Boat operators and chalet owners are located at Pengkalan Gawi, as is the DWNPPM where permits to enter Taman Negara must be obtained.

Tasik Kenyir has many attractions including waterfalls, isolated camps, fishing, rivers and rapids. The 38,000 hectare (95,000 acre) lake was created in 1985 when the waters were dammed for a massive hydroelectric system. The dam has resulted in the formation of hundreds of partially submerged islands. It is an angler's paradise and a nature lover's escape.

Transport across Tasik Kenyir to Tanjung Mentong and the Taman Negara Park Ranger Station is via boat only. Boats for hire are available on the foreshores of the lake.

Merapoh, Pahang

By Road
Merapoh, just south of Gua Musang, provides an alternative and quicker access to Gunung Tahan. The turn-off to the park is located on the Kuala Lipis to Gua Musang Road, about 20 kilometres (12 miles) south of Gua Musang. The road heads off the main road to the right (east) and the Ranger Station is located about 6 kilometres (4 miles) along a road that is accessible to most types of vehicles. The Ranger Station at Sungai Relau is as far as cars can drive and further access into the park is only permissible in park vehicles. Independent travellers can get off buses or taxis on the main road and either walk or try to get a lift for the remaining 6 kilometres (4 miles). The nearest main train station is Gua Musang and from here buses or taxis are available for the journey to the park turn-off.

Surviving Taman Negara

Things That Bite
The chances are that nothing will bite you while at Taman Negara, however, a few precautionary steps should be taken. Avoiding the problem is far better than seeking a cure, so visitors should be observant and be careful of what they touch.

Most forest mosquitoes and insects can be virtually eliminated through using insect repellents, wearing protective clothing and staying indoors around dusk.

Snakes and spiders can be harmful and should be shown respect if encountered. Urgent medical assistance should be sought if bitten.

Leeches are encountered in most lowland rainforests, so leech socks are a good investment. Leeches are not dangerous and should be pulled off and pressure applied to any bleeding.

Chemical insect repellents keep insects and leeches away, but they can be bad for the environment. Other preparations such as citronella oil or disinfectant mixed in baby oil, when rubbed onto the skin, are safe and effective alternatives.

King Cobra

What To Pack

Whenever entering an isolated natural area like Taman Negara it is always best to come self-sufficient and not depend upon others for equipment. This way, you have only yourself to blame when something goes wrong or you don't have another roll of film to capture that brilliant sunset on the river. While the park has shops that sell some equipment, areas like Kuala Koh are very isolated.

Unless visitors are engaging in specific adventure activities (like climbing Gunung Tahan) there is no need to pack specialised equipment like compasses, hiking boots etc. For visitors travelling to several parts of Malaysia there is no real need to pack additional equipment specifically for Taman Negara. The mini-mart at the Taman Negara Resort sells a good range of items.

A torch is always a useful piece of equipment, especially for caving and at Kuala Koh when the generator is switched off in the late evening. An inner sleeping sheet would also be beneficial at Kuala Koh. Leech socks, repellent, sunscreen, hat and mosquito coils are also essential items.

Most of the trails in the park are well defined and a pair of jogging/sport shoes will suffice as footwear. Sturdier hiking boots are a good idea for the longer treks.

Kit List

The following items will help make your visit more enjoyable:

- swimwear
- lightweight clothing
- walking shorts
- raincape
- hat
- sunscreen
- insect repellent
- water bottle
- torch
- camera (with plenty of film, spare battery, and flash)
- reading materials (entertainment is limited)
- money/credit cards (there are no banks)
- small souvenirs of your home country to hand out to those who help you
- survival first aid kit
- this guidebook

ENTRY FORMALITIES

All visitors to Taman Negara are required to complete an entry permit and pay a small fee. These are obtainable from DWNPPN Offices at the entrances to the park, offices in the nearest towns or from their HQ in Kuala Lumpur. Travellers on an organised tour will often have the fees incorporated in the tour costs, but each individual will have to complete an application form.

There is also a small charge for each camera and for a fishing license if needed.

Kuala Tahan, Pahang

There is little evidence of DWNPPN staff in the park as all guided walks are conducted by TNR or independent guides. These guides must carry visible identification with them at all times. The only contact visitors will have with staff is probably during the evening video show in the Interpretation Centre in the TNR. The video starts at

2045 but there is no time allocated for questions and answers. The static display in the Centre is very good and answers most questions visitors will have about the park. It is open from 0900-2130.

The DWNPPN Park HQ, open from 0900-2130, is located next to the mini-mart in the TNR.

Pahang – Kuala Tembeling
The office at the jetty at Kuala Tembeling is open daily from 0800-1615 but is often closed on Friday from 1300-1400 (although this is not clearly stated).

Kuala Koh – Kelantan
Offices are at Gua Musang or the Ranger Station at Kuala Koh.

Terengganu – Pengkalan Gawi (Tasik Kenyir) and Tanjung Mentong
Pengkalen Gawi is the nearest access point to the Terengganu side of Taman Negara. Gawi is located on the foreshores of Tasik Kenyir. Park officers are located in the main administrative office of the Tasik Kenyir Tourist Information Centre and Taman Negara visitor permits must be obtained here prior to crossing the lake. The Ranger Station is located just outside the park at Tanjung Mentong, some 90 minutes by boat from Pengkalan Gawi .

Merapoh – Pahang
The DWNPPN Ranger Station is located at Sungai Relau, some 6 kilometres (4 miles) off the Kuala Lipis to Gua Musang Road near the Pahang and Kelantan border. Access to Gunung Tahan from here is best sought beforehand to avoid disappointment. Enquiries should be directed to DWNPPN Headquarters in Kuala Lumpur or faxed directly to the Ranger Station at Sungai Relau.

Accommodation

Visitors to the park have several options, from comfortable resort-styled facilities at the TNR to tent camping at various camping grounds. Modern accommodation facilities with fresh piped water and electricity are available at the Park HQ. The style ranges from free-standing chalets to fully equipped hostels. A good selection of international and local food is available at various outlets around the Park HQ. Most of the hides within the park also have bunks for comfortable overnight stays.

The visitors' lodges at Kuala Keniam and Kuala Trenggan are equipped with crockery, cooking utensils, water, and firewood. There is also a simple restaurant.

The fishing lodges at Kuala Perkai and Lata Berkoh have basic facilities but visitors must come prepared as though for camping. There is a small charge.

Tents and camping equipment may be hired at Park HQ and a modest fee is charged for camping. Hikers and trekkers are advised to take extra emergency rations for any trek into the forest. There are tent campsites available at Kuala Tahan (100 sites), Kuala Keniam, various locations en route to Gunung Tahan and Lata Berkoh.

KUALA TAHAN

Taman Negara Resort (TNR)

Kuala Tahan
27000 Jerantut
Pahang
Tel : 09 2662200
Fax : 09 2663500

Most visitors to Taman Negara will stay in the TNR. This is the preferred accommodation for organised and packaged tours and is an excellent base from which to explore. The facilities are good and comfortable, having undergone recent refurbishment, and the service obliging, but remember it is not a city property so don't expect all that goes with urban hotels. The site overlooks the river with a backdrop of rainforest, and the landscaped gardens attract a number of feeding birds. There are several types of accommodation available, from hostel through to bungalow suites.

Bookings can be made in the Kuala Lumpur Sales Office (Tel: 03 2455585, Fax: 03 2455430, e-mail: taman_negararst@hotmail.com) or directly to the resort. They also manage Trenggan Lodge and Keniam Lodge.

The 110-room resort and 64-guest hostel is perched above the junction of the Tembeling and Tahan Rivers. There are no phones, and TV in only the most expensive chalets. Public phones and safe deposit boxes are located in the TNR reception area.

The TNR covers an area of six hectares (15 acres) and there are plans to develop this area with new chalets and facilities such as a swimming pool and spa/healthclub. In the evening animals come in from the forest and can be heard rooting around in the undergrowth searching for food.

Accommodation at TNR

Hostel: 8 beds/dormitory, ideal for those on a budget, ceiling fan, common bathrooms, rate includes breakfast at Teresek Cafeteria.

Guestroom: Adjoining brick units, air conditioned, attached bathroom, veranda, next to Teresek Cafeteria.

Chalet: mostly single chalets, some interconnecting, air conditioned, with bathroom.

Chalet Suite: Larger than chalet, air conditioned, attached bathroom, family room, veranda overlooking river or rainforest, minibar.

Bungalow Suite: Two bedrooms, attached bathrooms, family room with TV and video, kitchenette, mini bar, veranda over rainforest or river.

Kuala Trenggan (Terenggan) Lodge
Same contact address as the TNR

The lodge has a wonderful setting in the Tembeling Gorge, 9 kilometres (5½ miles) up the Sungai Tembeling from the TNR. There are ten wooden chalets providing beds and bedding, eating utensils, kerosene stove, lanterns, water and a restaurant serving basic meals. The lodge is 45 minutes by boat or five hours walk from the TNR.

Kuala Keniam (Kenyam) Lodge
Same contact address as the TNR

The lodge is located at the furthest outpost of the Pahang accommodation facilities. There are ten wooden chalets, and the boat journey takes about two hours from the TNR or 1.5 days on foot with a stop over at Kuala Trenggan for the night. The facilities are the same as those at Kuala Trenggan. Camping is also available here.

Hides
Same contact address as the TNR

There are several hides in the park – called 'bumbun' in Bahasa. All but Bumbun Tahan provide simple accommodation for overnight stays at a modest fee. The number of beds available at each hide are as follows: Yong (8); Belau (6); Cegar Anjing (8); Tabing (8); Kumbang (6); and Tahan (0). Tahan Hide is located just 70 metres (80 yards) behind the TNR with the entrance path being located between chalets 89 and 90.

Visitors who are really keen to see the nocturnal activities of animals should plan to stay a night in a hide, though facilities are rustic. All hides except Tahan are equipped with bush toilets. Cooking is not permitted in the hides. Bedsheets are available from the TNR.

Most hides are accessible by boat and/or walking. Boat trips are quicker and more expensive, with little walking involved (except for Bumbun Kumbang which is a boat trip and a 40-minute walk).

Nusa Camp
Kuala Tahan
27000 Jerantut
Tel : 09 2663043, Fax : 09 2664369
Budget accommodation is available at this location just 15 minutes boat ride upstream from Kuala

Tapir

31

TAMAN NEGARA

Tahan on the opposite side of the river to the park. There are 16 A-frame chalets, 10 hostels and a camping ground. A restaurant overlooking the river serves local food at reasonable prices. There are guided tours to all parts of the park and boats to and from Park HQ and other parts of the park.

Lata Berkoh

On the banks of the Sungai Tahan this fishing lodge provides rudimentary shelter and facilities. Accommodation fees are modest and the lodge is equipped with beds and mattresses, but visitors must bring bedding, food and cooking utensils.

Walking to hides

Walking times for each hide from Park HQ are approximately:

Yong	2 hours
Belau	90 minutes
Cegar Anjing	75 minutes
Tabing	75 minutes
Kumbang	5 hours
Tahan	10 minutes

Kuala Perkai

Provides basic facilities on the Sungai Tembeling, similar to those at Lata Berkoh.

Agoh Chalet

Kuala Tahan
Tel/Fax : 09 2967006
6 chalets (each sleeping 2) moderate fee; 10 hostel rooms (4/room) budget fee, fans, no restaurant but features the 'Jungle Bus' for night animal spotting safaris.

Ekotone Chalet

Kuala Tahan
Tel : 010 9888932, Fax : 09 2776652
8 chalets (each sleeping 2, AC, bathroom) high/moderate fee; hostel rooms (8 room, fan) budget fee. Quiet location, neat gardens, pay phone, laundry, recreational room and restaurant.

Liana Hostel and Restaurant Terapong

Kuala Tahan
Tel: 09 2669322
No frills accommodation with10 rooms, each with 4 bunks at budget fee. The hostel is associated with one of the floating restaurants on the river and it has a good view of the river junction. Rooms are fan-cooled, no on-site food but drinks are available.

Tembeling Riverview Hostel and Chalets

Kuala Tahan
Tel: 09 2666766

32

9 chalets (each sleeping 2 or 3, fan) moderate fees and hostel beds at a budget fee. Mosquito nets and towels included. Restaurant (Chinese, *halal*) overlooking river, tours organised from here. Garden hammocks allow guests to take in the view.

Teresek View Village
Kuala Tahan
Tel: 011 911742, 011 911494
Fax: 09 2776184.
12 chalets with fans at a moderate fee, 3 with AC at a higher fee and hostel beds at a budget fee. Mini-mart, souvenir shop, pay phone, restaurant opposite and minibus transfers to Jerantut available.

Kuala Koh, Kelantan
The only accommodation in the park here is operated by the National Parks. There are both moderately priced chalets and 40 budget dormitory beds from which to choose. The 6 chalets have 2 beds each and have fans, cold water showers, electricity (from 1800 to 2300 hours) and toilets. They are comfortable and have a pleasant setting near the river. An adjoining canteen serves simple but adequate meals. For a small fee any fish you catch can be cooked.

Tasik Kenyir, Terengganu
Around Tasik Kenyir there are several established resorts and chalets outside the park. Tasik Kenyir Resort (Tel: 09 6668888, Fax: 09 6668344) offers good resort facilities close to Pengkalan Gawi. Most other places to stay on the lake are chalets floating on pontoons.

In the Terengganu side of the park there are several camping grounds at Sungai Cacing and Sungai Petang. These are popular with fishing enthusiasts and groups since they offer easy access to the park's prime fishing sites.

Merapoh, Pahang
Camping is possible at the Ranger Station at Sungai Relau for a minimal fee. Campers should bring their own tents and camping equipment.

PROTECTING THE PARK
The National Park is protected and everyone visiting Taman Negara and other natural places in Malaysia has an important role to play in ensuring they stay this way for present and future visitors. Many of the following rules and guidelines are obvious to most people, but there may still be some who need to be reminded.

Changes to the rainforest ecosystem have been kept to a minimum and once visitors move away from Kuala Tahan, there is little evidence of any development or disturbance to be seen.

All plants and animals are protected in the park and even the smallest change can have a big impact upon plant and animal communities that have evolved in isolation for centuries.

Protect the Park

1. Observe all park rules that are clearly displayed in the park. Do not destroy or remove any plant or animal. The cumulative effect of others doing this does have an impact. It is an offence to remove plants, animals and to shoot, trap and/or collect animals.

2. Leave the park cleaner than you found it. Dispose of rubbish appropriately and clean up, if need be, after those who don't understand the need for a litter-free forest. All drinks containers sold at the TNR come with a deposit to encourage recycling.

3. Pets are not allowed into Taman Negara as they may introduce diseases to isolated populations or may escape and go wild.

4. Leave radios and cassette players at home as the music not only disturbs the wildlife but also those who want to see it. Be considerate of other visitors who may be engaging in activities like birdwatching and animal spotting that require silence.

5. Do not feed or leave food out for wild animals. Encouraging them only makes them aggressive scavengers and a nuisance to people.

6. Glass containers are prohibited in areas of the park away from the TNR.

7. Avoid buying and taking excessively packaged products into the park as the waste has to be disposed of somewhere. Take as little as possible on walks and return all rubbish to Park HQ and place in a bin (recycling bin where possible).

This simple code makes a difference in preserving natural areas like Taman Negara.

Visitors Can Play A Role In Taman Negara

The joint objectives of conservation and rural development in Taman Negara require the commitment of both visitors and participants in the tourism industry. All parties can take on a more active role to minimize negative impacts and adopt more sustainable practices. Tourists can contribute by making discerning choices before and during the trip, and by providing feedback afterwards. In addition, ensuring that local people benefit from tourism creates an incentive for them to preserve natural habitats. Environmentally responsible nature tourism involves:

- *travel to undisturbed areas to appreciate their natural and cultural features.*

- *minimal visitor impact on the natural and social surroundings.*

- *only development that does not exhaust or degrade the resource upon which it depends.*

- *promoting and supporting conservation efforts in the host area.*

- *providing opportunities for the beneficial involvement of local communities.*

Guides

There are many guides offering their services in and around the park. All tourism guides in Malaysia have to be registered and carry their registration with them while they are working. The TNR has professional guiding services available at set rates and all visitors should at least go on one day walk and one evening walk to learn more about the rainforest ecosystem.

Walkers should never venture off trails on their own and all walkers going on extended walks should engage the services of an experienced guide and inform the authorities when they intend to return from their walk.

Slow Loris

FOOD AND EATING

In Malaysia, one of the closest things to a national pastime is eating and Malaysians will often greet visitors and guests with *sudah makan?* or 'have you eaten?' If you haven't, food and/or drinks will often be organised.

One of the delights of Malaysia is eating, so sit back and enjoy. Many Malaysians will eat frequently but usually in small portions. Breakfast, lunch and dinner are taken, in addition to snacks during the day and evening.

The main culinary styles are Malay, Chinese and Indian. In the large cities other Asian and Western styles are available.

Most large establishments add a 10% service charge and there is a 5% Government tax. These may be added into the bill or indicated as '++'. Tipping therefore, is not considered appropriate unless a staff member has been particularly helpful, efficient and courteous.

There are special practices observed by various groups within the country, and a little understanding will prevent embarrassment. For mostly religious and health reasons, various groups of people do not eat pork and/or beef. The term *halal* means that pork or its bi-products have not been used in the food or in the preparation. *Makanan halal* indicates that a restaurant or shop is a pork-free outlet. In Taman Negara, most meals are *halal.*

Kuala Tahan

In Kuala Tahan the range of culinary delights is limited but there is sufficient variety to keep even the most demanding diner happy. A mini-mart also provides snack food and cool drinks from 0800 – 2300 daily. Sensibly, there is a small deposit on all drink containers to encourage visitors to return them for recycling.

At the TNR the Teresek Cafeteria and the Tahan Restaurant both serve *halal*

35

TAMAN NEGARA

Malaysian and international dishes. The cafeteria is often booked out by large groups and conventions and meals are then taken in the Tahan Restaurant.

Buffets are the normal fare for most meals at the Tahan Restaurant, although there is also a menu. Children pay about half the adult rate. Visitors on a package deal will normally have all meals included. Drinks are best consumed in the Tembeling Lounge or the Tahan restaurant and adjoining garden area, although alcohol can be hard to purchase.

Immediately opposite the TNR are several floating restaurants which offer a variety of Malaysian and Western dishes at substantial discounts to the TNR. These pleasant, airy restaurants are reached by a small punt which crosses the river from 0730 – 2300. There are also restaurants at both Kuala Keniam and Kuala Trenggan serving basic dishes but with little variety.

Kuala Koh

There is a small canteen serving simple village food and drinks. The meals are dominated by rice, vegetables, fish and chicken, and are sustaining. Like at most Malaysian destinations, the prices are very reasonable. Staff will gladly cook any fish caught in the local rivers. This is not gourmet dining and no alcohol is served. Visitors with specific culinary passions or requirements should bring their own food and drink from town.

Terengganu

There are no food outlets on the Terengganu side of Taman Negara and all food must be brought in. The nearest restaurants and shops are located at Pengkalan Gawi at the head of Tasik Kenyir.

Merapoh, Pahang

No food is available at the Ranger Station at Sungai Relau. The nearest shops and restaurants are 6 kilometres (4 miles) back along the road to the Merapoh township.

Minimal Impact Code

• The natural areas of Malaysia have many rare and endangered plants and animals. It is important that you do not harm, disturb or remove any of them.

• Do not encourage trade in living plants or animals, or items produced from threatened natural resources.

• When walking, stay on identifiable paths and follow your guide.

• When near animals, avoid making undue noise or movement, or doing anything to disturb them. Use binoculars rather than trying to get too close.

By assisting in these small ways, you will help to promote responsible tourism for the future. Remember, you are one of the fortunate few who has the opportunity to visit this place. Don't spoil the experience for others.

Take nothing but photographs and fond memories, leave nothing but footprints and smiling faces.

THE PARK'S BOATMEN NAVIGATE THEIR CRAFT SKILFULLY ALONG THE SOMETIMES TURBULENT WATERWAYS.

FOR MORE ACTIVE VISITORS, THE PARK'S LONGER TRAILS OFFERS AN AUTHENTIC JUNGLE ADVENTURE.

WHITEWATER RAFTING ALONG THE POWERFUL RAPIDS OF THE SUNGAI TEMBELING IS AN EXHILARATING EXPERIENCE FOR THE MORE ADVENTUROUS.

LEFT: AT NIGHT THE FOREST COMES ALIVE, AND ON SPOTLIT GUIDED WALKS FROM THE CAMPS VISITORS MAY ENCOUNTER A HOST OF NOCTURNAL CREATURES SELDOM SEEN BY DAY.

OPPOSITE ABOVE: SUNGAI KENIAM IS ONE OF THE MOST POPULAR SPOTS FOR FISHING AND OFFERS THE ANGLER THE IRRESISTABLE CHALLENGE OF LANDING A PRIZED KELAH.

OPPOSITE BELOW: THE TRAIL TO LATAH BERKOH IS A PLEASANT DAY'S RETURN WALK FROM TAMAN NEGARA RESORT, OR ALTERNATIVELY A SHORT TRIP BY RIVER BOAT.

AT THE LATA BERKOH CASCADES VISITORS MAY COOL OFF IN THE DEEP POOL BELOW THE FALLS.

Activities and Adventure

Taman Negara has a range of action and adventure to suit everybody, from serious sports enthusiasts through to the armchair adventurer. Most activities revolve around trekking through the rainforest but there are limestone caves to be explored, rapids to be shot, canopy walks to be climbed, fish waiting to be caught and mountains to be scaled.

The boat ride into the park is an adventure in itself. Visitors can immerse themselves in the many sights, sounds and smells of the park. Jungle trails can be undertaken both in the day and at night, giving the visitor an insight into the natural wonders of the rainforest. The amazing canopy walk gives an alternative view of forest life, from the abundance of epiphytic plants to the canopy birdlife. Visitors can also relax around and swim in the beautiful pools and rivers found along many of the trails. The ancient rainforests of Taman Negara provide a sensory journey deep into the natural heart of Malaysia.

Trekking

Visitors to Taman Negara have only two options for moving about and seeing things – by boat or on foot. Apart from river boating, trekking is the most popular activity in the park.

Trekking in Taman Negara doesn't require any great skill, fitness or equipment unless overnight treks are planned. There are walks of various durations, ranging from an hour's stroll to a nine day climb to the summit of Gunung Tahan. Climbs like the latter should not be undertaken lightly as they require fitness, preparation, equipment and good guiding. Most park visitors will participate in treks of a few hours maximum and these can be attempted by most fit people. The river offers a pleasant alternative for those who can't or don't want to return from their destination on foot.

Good walking shoes are essential and, in most instances, sneakers are more than adequate. Since Taman Negara is a rainforest you should always be prepared to get wet. The biggest problems for most walkers are heat and humidity, so drinking water is essential. On long walks it is always a good idea to drink as much water as possible prior to departure. The high humidity may also result in excessive salt loss through perspiration, so trekkers also need to replace lost body salts.

To keep cool, wear lightweight clothing and a hat. Another possible irritant is insects, and in really wet weather, leeches (see General Health, page 14). Fortunately, none of them will cause long term damage, so relax and enjoy the walk.

River Trips

The main river systems on the Pahang side of the park are the Tembeling, Tahan, Trenggan, Keniam and Relai-Aring-Lebir. Boat trips start from Park HQ at Kuala Tahan.

Kuala Koh is on the upper reaches of the Lebir River and its tributaries – the Badung, Pertang and Koh. Boat trips, mostly for fishing, can be arranged up these narrow rivers. On the Terengganu side of the park, boats are the only way to reach the various attractions such as caves, fishing locations, waterfalls and trails. These trips are made across Tasik Kenyir and along some of the tributaries. Permission needs to be obtained from Park HQ to enter some of the once popular fishing streams like Sungai Cacing.

Short-clawed Otter

Gone fishing

Most fishing in Taman Negara is done with artificial lures on a reel although local fruits can be used during the fruiting season. The recommended fishing gear depends upon the kind of fish you're after. The following is a rough guideline:

2-5 kilogram (4-11 pound) lines for *lampam, daun, rong, tapah bemban*
6-9 kilogram (13-20 pound) for *tengas, kelisa, sebarau*, small *kelah*
9-12 kilogram (20-26 pound) for big *kelah, seberau* and *toman*

Kelisa are one of the best sporting fish as they put up a great struggle and leap high out of the water. They prefer deep water, areas where there is debris and where the bank is indented.

While whitewater rafting is popular in many parts of the world, the rapids and cascades of Taman Negara are not that big and adventurous. However, they are mostly safe for all ages and to 'shoot' the rapids does not take any special skill or equipment – just sit back in a sampan and let the boatman do the work.

The jetboats from Tembeling up to Kuala Tahan are also thrilling – though the speed of the boats is restricted for safety and to avoid environmental disturbance.

Fishing

Fishing is a popular recreational activity in most parts of the park, especially the Kuala Koh and Terengganu access points. Sungai Keniam, upstream from Kuala Tahan is one of the most popular fishing locations on the Pahang side. Perkai Lodge is also a good spot and mainly attracts fishing folk. Downstream from the cataracts at Lata Berkoh on Sungai Tahan there are several good deep fishing holes.

Permits are required for fishing in all the rivers of the park and may be obtained from Park HQ for a modest fee when visitors register to enter the park. Fishing traps are not permitted in Taman Negara.

On the Kuala Tahan side of the park, fishing is restricted to Sungai Tahan below Lata Berkoh and Sungai Keniam below Kuala Keniam Kecil. The most suitable months for fishing are the drier months of February to April and July and August. At other times, local rainfall may disturb the fishing.

There are over 200 species of fish in the rivers, with the most popular for anglers being the *kelah* (Malaysian Mahseer), the *sebarau* (Malaysian Jungle Perch), the *tengas* (Brook Carp), the *toman* (Greater Snakehead) and *baung* (various species of catfish).

From Kuala Koh Ranger Station fishing is good upstream on Sungai Lebir and Sungai Pertang. Both rivers are accessible during the dry season but during the monsoon (end of October to end of January) boating is usually not possible due to the fast flow. Boats may be hired from the Ranger Station staff for which there is a daily charge for up to 3 people per boat. They also have fishing guides and camping equipment for hire. The journey up the river passes through some rapids, limestone cliffs and overhanging rainforest trees. There are several sandy banks and some deep holes, especially Lubuk Kaloi and Lubuk Kedah, that are very good fishing spots.

Fishing is the main activity in the Taman Negara waters of Tasik Kenyir on the Terengganu side. Sungai Cacing was once the most popular spot but it is no longer possible as the waters are protected for breeding purposes. Fishing boat charter is possible from various operators at the settlement of Pengkalan Gawi on Tasik Kenyir.

Swimming

There are many good swimming holes in all four access sides to Taman Negara. In Bahasa Malaysia, these are called *lubuk,* but there are many other parts of the rivers that offer good swimming opportunities. Caution needs to be exercised, especially near rapids where there may be strong and dangerous currents. The rivers should not be used during periods of flooding.

Sungai Tembeling is not considered the best as the current is strong and the water is not clear. But there are several operators offering tyre tube floats for a relaxed and safe way of floating down parts of the river. Life jackets are also provided.

The best swimming rivers on the Pahang side are the tributaries of the Tembeling such as the Tahan, Trenngan, Keniam and Perkai. The waters here are clear despite being slightly brownish and there are swimming holes of varied depths. The rapids at Lata Berkoh are very good for a natural jacuzzi. Two swimming holes, Lubuk Simpon (20 minutes from Kuala Tahan) and Lubuk Lesong (two hours from Kuala Tahan), both on the Sungai Tahan, are considered the best and most accessible swimming locations.

Climbing

Gunung Tahan, the highest peak on Peninsular Malaysia at 2,187 metres (7,173 feet), is located in the park but the climb does not require specialised mountaineering or sports climbing equipment or preparation.

The trail between Kuala Trenggan and Kuala Keniam has a few limestone rises that can be climbed. Along the trail at the north-east corner of Batu Luas the trail links with the path from Kuala Keniam. Here, at the base of a limestone cliff, there is a camp beside Sungai Luas.

The large cave, Daun Menari, is situated near the cliff base a little distance away and there is a 30 minute walk along the base of the outcrop. Here there are at least two climbs to the top of Batu Luas. One starts a few hundred metres south of the campsite and the other from just

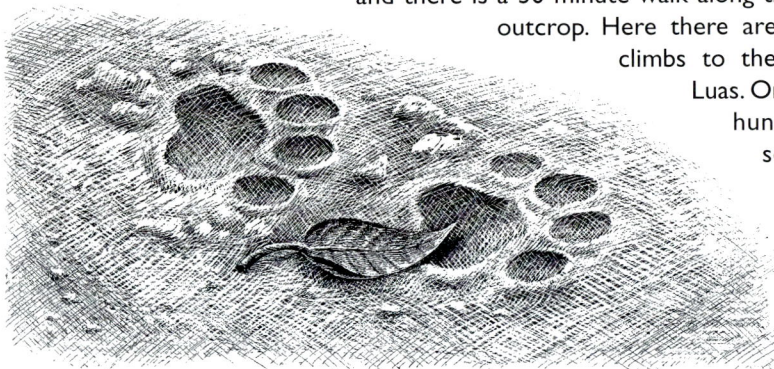

Tiger tracks

beyond the entrance to Gua Daun Menari. While no special equipment is required, the ascent should only be attempted by fit climbers carrying lots of water, as it is exhausting in the heat.

Caving

There are many caves (*gua* in Bahasa Malaysia) in the park. These have mostly been sculptured by underground rivers flowing through limestone outcrops. The caves are home to various bats, racer snakes and insects. Visitors should come prepared with torches and seek the services of a good guide as they are not places to become lost in. Torches can be hired from the TNR or purchased from the mini-mart.

Gua Telinga is located 2.6 kilometres (1.6 miles), within one hour's walk or ten minutes boat trip from Kuala Tahan. The return walk from the riverbank to the cave takes about one hour.

From Kuala Keniam Lodge visitors can explore the Gua Duan Menari (Cave of the Dancing Leaves), Gua Luas and Gua Kepayang. The caves are located in an isolated area of the park, 2½ hours boat ride from Kuala Tahan.

Serious cavers can explore some of the more distant caves in the park. Expeditions are often mounted by such cavers, many of whom belong to MNS. Interested cavers looking to join such expeditions should contact MNS for further details.

Wildlife Watching

Choosing the right time of day and year is very important for spotting wildlife. Like humans, many animals avoid the heat of the day, so early morning (0600-0900) and late afternoon (1700-1900) are the best times for diurnal animals. The main flowering and fruiting season from March to October is a good time for spotting animals feeding, and this period also coincides with more favourable weather. Large areas of half eaten fruit along the tracks are an indication that something is in the upper storeys of the rainforest. Droppings on the trail are another important sign.

Some animals, like lizards and snakes, like to bask in open sunny areas, but within the rainforest these areas can be quite limited. Forest trails, especially those near open riverbanks, are good locations to see such reptiles.

Animals are easily startled by noise so it is best to keep as quiet as possible. Binoculars are always useful. Remember to use appropriate protection from the sun. Lightweight and dull-coloured clothing are recommended for walking through the jungle. Since rain is one of the features of rainforests, a raincoat may come in handy!

Taman Negara is not the Plains of the Serengeti, nor are animals as visible as on the open Savannah of Africa since the rainforest provides a wonderful habitat for animals to camouflage themselves. Sightings of large mammals are consequently rare. However, with luck, mammals may be seen at one of the several hides in the park, where patient visitors can sit and wait for the wildlife to be attracted to the mineral rich salt licks. A good torch is essential for night spotting as the first things most people will see are the eyes reflecting in the beam of light. Slow casting of the beam across the salt lick often reveals something, be it a Tapir, deer, or pig. Even Seladang have been sighted at Bumbun Kumbang where it is a little more open.

Another good way to see nocturnal animals is to go spotlighting with a guide who has a reasonably powerful spot. The most popular trail for guided walks from the TNR heads in the general direction of the Canopy Walk. While the trail is never really crowded, serious spot-lighters may want to set off in any other direction. Head mounted spotlights can bring the best results.

Butterflies are another beautiful component of the rainforest ecosystem. Lepidopterists have over 900 species to see in the forests. Leave these colourful specimens for others to see and appreciate. Do not catch or collect them.

Hints for birders

Birdwatching in dense forest can be frustrating. To improve your chances:

- Stop and wait quietly for birds to come to you.
- Be alert for sound and movement
- Check fruiting/flowering forest trees.
- Check riverbanks, ponds, salt licks
- Wear neutral-coloured clothing
- Keep quiet
- Early morning is the best time for birds

Birdwatching

First-time birdwatchers in Taman Negara often get very excited about the bird numbers they expect to find in the rainforest environment. However, it should be remembered that birdwatching is not easy in the dense rainforest and birdwatchers need to be quiet, patient and alert. On trails it is often best to pause for a while and wait quietly for the birds to come to you. A seemingly silent forest can suddenly come to life when a mixed feeding party passes through.

Most birdwatchers will already know exactly what is required to make the most of their pastime. For those with just a passing interest, binoculars and a good field guide are essential (see *Further Reading* page 123). Binoculars with 7 times magnification are generally adequate for Taman Negara. Telescopes are more powerful but can be hard to use in the forest. To identify species back at camp, a note book is useful to record identifying features such as size, colour, habitat, time of day, location etc.

Look for birds where they drink or feed, such as on any fruiting or flowering forest trees. The riverbanks, ponds and salt licks are another good location. Some of the best trails are those to Bukit Teresek (Crestless Fireback Pheasant, Argus Pheasant, pittas and Malaysian Rail Babbler), Sungai Tahan (Lesser Fish-eagle, Black and Red Broadbill and Masked Finfoot), Gua Telinga(swiftlets and White-crowned Forktail), the open banks opposite the TNR (Black-thighed Falconet) and the boat journey from Tembeling to Kuala Tahan (eagles, kingfishers, swifts and swallows).

Operators like Kingfisher Tours (see *Address Book*) offer special trips for birders.

Plant Spotting

Visitors to Taman Negara don't have to travel far to see forests and plants. The TNR is located in dense lowland tropical forests and any walk within a few metres of the perimeter of the resort enters the trees. Visitors often need their 'eyes opened' before they spot anything in the forest. The best people to do this are the local guides for whom the forest is home. A guided walk in a small group is highly recommended.

There are several plant communities that should be seen while in the park. The Canopy Walk high above the forest floor is spectacular. The journey up the Sungai Tahan is another 'must'. The montane forests are unusual considering their tropical location, but to see them visitors must undertake the full nine day Gunung Tahan trek.

Photography

Few tourists these days travel without a still or video camera. Most Malaysians are relaxed about being photographed, although it is inappropriate to thrust cameras in people's faces. Unless you can take photos from a distance with a long lens it is always polite to ask permission to photograph anybody. Many Malaysians enjoy being photographed although the Orang Asli may show little interest. Taking pictures in such circumstances may require some perseverance, patience and perhaps a little theatrics to convey your wishes.

There are no photographic treks to Taman Negara organised from within the country but international photo magazines often advertise specialised organised photographic tours to Malaysia.

It is wise to be well equipped in the rainforest. However, carrying too much can be a nuisance, so getting the right balance is important. Sometimes porters can be hired to carry equipment. While there is a loss in picture quality with many zoom lenses, they do save on weight. Longer lenses (e.g. 200mm) are good for taking wildlife, people and distance shots. A small tripod is useful in low light situations inside the rainforest or caves. Alternatively, take a flash and/or fast film.

A polarising filter can be helpful, and for overcast skies graduated blue and yellow filters are useful. Bring spare batteries as they and other equipment are not widely available in Taman Negara. Facilities for repairs are only available in Kuala Lumpur.

Choosing slide or print film depends upon how the photographs will be used. It is expensive to obtain prints from slides but almost impossible to get good slides from prints. The light in Malaysia is mostly good and film speed selection need not be higher than 200 ISO. The exception is in rainforest where the light is often poor. The light is generally best just after sunrise and just before sunset, when it is low and golden. Midday light is intense and generally not suitable for photography. Print film is readily available in Malaysia and Taman Negara, however slide film is more scarce and is not sold in the

Banded Pitta

park. Photographers are generally advised to bring their own film.

The guides in the park are normally very good at accommodating the needs of special interest groups such as photographers. Some boat drivers are keen to get from A to B as quickly as possible, but for those who specifically want to photograph rainforest features along the way, the guides are normally obliging. Chartering a whole boat will guarantee that photographers can take the photos they like, when they like.

Scientific Projects

Most of the scientific projects conducted in Taman Negara are those done by government departments or local universities. Scientists interested in research projects and visits should direct their enquires to DWNPPN well in advance as permission needs to be granted, and this could take some time.

The Forest Research Institute of Malaysia (FRIM) should also be contacted regarding research opportunities.

ADJACENT PLACES OF INTEREST

Terengganu – Tasik Kenyir

Tasik (Lake) Kenyir is the largest dammed lake in South East Asia. It was created by building the Sultan Mahmud Dam and flooding several rivers of inland Terengganu State.

At the far end of the dam lies the Terengganu access to Taman Negara. There is no obvious park boundary and visitors to Tasik Kenyir travel into Taman Negara to look at limestone caves, waterfalls, for fishing and to go jungle trekking. However many visitors to this part of Malaysia come to see the lake rather than the national park.

Parts of Tasik Kenyir have a rather eerie feeling in that hundreds of dead trees emerge from the water. It is a like a jungle graveyard created when the forest was drowned by the rising dam waters and the grey stumps and branches give the lake a distinct atmosphere. While some are now being logged from beneath the water others provide important perches for birds and spawning grounds for fish.

Around the lake there are several camping sites, resorts (one even has a golf course), trails and waterfalls. The waterfalls are popular with locals who come here to relax, picnic, swim and camp. The most visited waterfalls are Lasir, Saok and Tembat. Fishing is the other popular attraction and various species have been introduced to encourage the sport. There are several boats available for chartering to the best fishing locations.

While few visitors enter the Terengganu side of the park, there are a range of activities and accommodation options around Tasik Kenyir to justify a visit of a few days.

Pahang – Krau Game Reserve

The 55,000 hectare (136,000 acre) Krau Game Reserve was established in 1923, before Taman Negara. The area includes lowland rainforest as well as montane oak forest. The animals here are similar to those in Taman Negara although the reserve was specifically established to provide a habitat for the Seladang. Deer and pheasant breeding programmes have also been carried out here.

Life in The Forest

The rainforest ecosystem is one of the most diverse in the world. It is rich in plant and animal species that have adapted to its unique environmental conditions. In Malaysia there are an estimated 12,500 species of flowering plants. Many of the plant species found in Taman Negara have economic, technological or social value, while others may have uses yet to be discovered. Several of these plant species are endemic to the park.

Animal life within Taman Negara is just as spectacular, although sometimes a little difficult to see. As well as a variety of mammals, over 275 species of bird have been recorded within the boundaries of the park. Insect life is abundant, with many dazzling species of butterfly and beetle to be seen, especially in the more open areas or on the banks of rivers and pools.

Life in the forest is like a fascinating and complex ecological jigsaw puzzle. A little knowledge of how it all fits together helps the visitor to appreciate the true wonders of the park.

Habitats and Terrains

There are various distinct plant communities within Taman Negara. The prevelance of each community partly depends upon topography, and is influenced by such factors as altitude and drainage. Mixed lowland dipterocarp forest is the most common, covering 60% of the park, although it is replaced in some areas due to particular environmental factors. Along the rivers there is a distinct riverine community. Montane forests of oaks, laurels, rattans, palms and conifers appear at altitudes of 750 metres (2,500 feet) and above. Above 1,500 metres (5,000 feet) there is a band of cloud forest, and on the summit of Gunung Tahan, dwarf montane vegetation is evident.

Mixed Lowland Dipterocarp Forests

The Dipterocarpaceae family is one of the most important plant families in Malaysia and dominates the mixed lowland and hill forests in the country. At one stage, dipterocarp forests made up 85% of all forested land and this once covered 58% of the total landmass. Although development has done much damage elsewhere, in Taman Negara these forests are effectively protected.

There are 155 species in the family in Peninsular Malaysia and many are important sources of saleable hardwood timber. This forest type is also rich in wild fruit species, with about 10% of the trees here bearing edible fruits such as durian and petai (a long green pea-like pod).

'Di' means two, 'ptero' means wing and 'carp' means seed, so dipterocarp means seeds with two wings (although the problem with this name is that not all species have two wings; some have five and others have none). The wings allow the seeds to be dispersed by wind or water. Individual dipterocarp trees can produce up to 4 million flowers in two weeks – but each flower only lasts a day. Plants of the Shorea family are among the most commonly found dipterocarps.

Limestone Hills

The vegetation that develops on limestone rich parent material is strikingly different from the surrounding vegetation. The topography comprises sheer sided cliffs with serrated summits and the vegetation clings to the exposed rocky surface. Gua Peningat in Taman Negara reaches an altitude of 713 metres (2,339 feet). Limestone vegetation is ecologically important as it contains a disproportionately high number of species for the limited area it covers. In Peninsular Malaysia, for example, 13% of flowering plants and ferns are found on the 0.3% of total land surface occupied by limestone vegetation.

Bamboo Forests

Bamboo is a grass, which in Taman Negara occurs mainly in disturbed areas. The 80 species of bamboo found in Malaysia are some of the most useful plants to people as they can be used in construction, handicrafts, food, musical instruments, cooking and raft making. Bamboo clumps are common along the trail to the Canopy Walk.

Riverine Forests

The riverine environment, particularly along the Sungai Tahan, is one of the more accessible and impressive sights of Taman Negara. The huge *Neram* trees (*Dipterocarpus oblongifolius*) overhang and join here to give the impression for river travellers of boating through a tunnel of greenery. Hornbills and kingfishers are common bird inhabitants of this environment

Montane Forest

Altitude is an important variable for plant growth in Taman Negara. The higher the altitude, the cooler the climate, and though the temperature variation is not high it is enough to significantly change the vegetation composition and structure. With altitude, the height of the trees reduces, and buttress roots, large woody climbers and cauliflory become uncommon.

The lower montane forest occurs up to altitudes of approximately 1,800 metres (6,000 feet) and Oak and Laurel family plants are common.

Upper montane forests occur from 1,800 metres (6,000) to almost 3,000 metres (10,000 feet) and are notable for their substantially lower canopy, at less than 18 metres (60 feet). Orchids and ferns are less abundant but mosses, lichens and liverworts are common. The lush green appearance of the tree trunks has led to the forests also being called mossy forests.

On the summit of Gunung Tahan, dwarf upper montane (ericaceous) forests are dominated by palm species such as the endemic palm *Livingstonia tahanensis*. Other plants are gnarled and wind-etched due to constant exposure to high winds and low temperatures.

Forest layers

Rainforest vegetation is stratified by height into five main canopy layers, each of which provides separate niches for plants and animals.

1. The emergent layer: 40–45 metres (132–148 feet)
2. The main storey: 20–30 metres (66–99 feet)
3. The understorey: up to 20 metres (66 feet)
4. The shrub layer: up to 5 metres (16 feet)
5. The forest floor: ground level

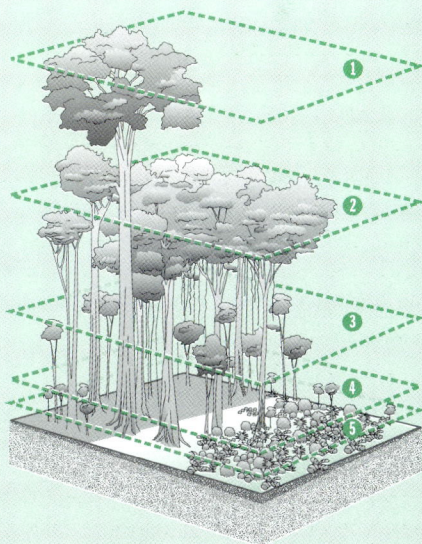

PLANT COMMUNITIES

Layers

The rainforest is divided into several distinct vertical layers: emergents, canopy, upper storey, middle storey, understorey and ground plants. Gaining an impression of all the layers is not always possible but the Canopy Walk at Kuala Tahan is a good place to start, as the walk winds its way through much of the middle and upper storeys of the forest. Riverbanks are not always good places as the higher incidence of light gives an unfair advantage to climbing plants such as creepers, vines and lianas,.

The tallest tree species in Malaysia is the *Koompassia excelsa* or locally called, *Tualang*. This spectacular tree can grow to a height of 80 metres (260 feet) with an average of about 50 metres (160 feet). It is commonly found in lowland forests and normally seen as an emergent rising above the canopy of Taman Negara.

Buttress Roots

The heavy rainfall within rainforest ecosystems leaches essential elements from the upper soil levels. In order to obtain nutrients many rainforest trees have a shallow root system. Buttress roots are an adaptation that enables trees to obtain nutrients while still providing strength so that the tree will not topple over.

Cauliflory

Many trees in dipterocarp forests exhibit a cauliflorous property. This means that fruits and flowers are found growing directly from the tree trunk.

Flowering

The favourable climatic conditions of Taman Negara are ideal for year round plant growth. However, there are only a few plants that flower regularly and continuously throughout the year. Dipterocarps, for example, may flower heavily and then there may be no more flowering for another two to five years. Scientists believe this is the result of climatic factors, but they cannot isolate one variable. For trees that flower annually, the onset of the drier months (January–July in Taman Negara) is the beginning of the flowering season.

Epiphytes

Epiphytes are plants that live attached to another living plant. Unlike parasites, that tap the nutrients from another plant in order to survive, epiphytes obtain nutrients from decaying matter that accumu-

Rattans

Rattans use sharp barbs to gain a purchase on trees to facilitate their climb. These barbs also protect the plant from hungry herbivores. Rattan is economically important in Malaysia but great skill and care is required in harvesting this spikey plant. Some 20 species of rattans are used for weaving baskets, building materials, mats and rope.

Beware: these barbs also seem to be attracted to passing hikers and their clothing.

Altitudinal zonation

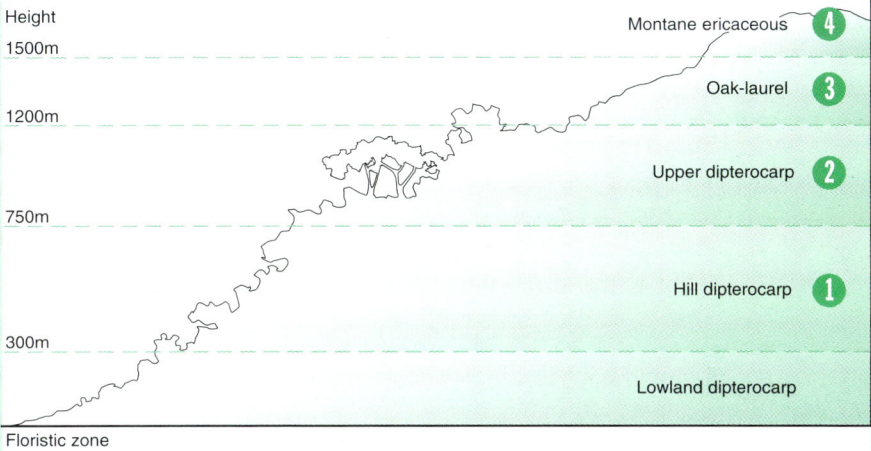

Height
1500m

Montane ericaceous ④

Oak-laurel ③

1200m

Upper dipterocarp ②

750m

Hill dipterocarp ①

300m

Lowland dipterocarp

Floristic zone

lates around plant roots and from rainfall. Epiphytes can be found in all layers of the rainforest but are more common in the canopy. Bird's Nest Fern (*Asplenium nidus*) and Stag's Horn Fern (*Platycerium coronarium*) are common epiphytes in Taman Negara.

Some orchids are also epiphytic. The Orchidaceae family is by far Malaysia's largest plant family, with over 850 species in Peninsular Malaysia alone.

Vines and Lianas

Climbing vines and lianas are an integral part of the tropical rainforest and in a way, hold the forest together. One of the essential elements for plant growth is sunlight and most plants in the rainforest reach for this life-giving element. Climbing vines and lianas twist and curl their way to the top layers of the forest using other stronger plants as their support. They also provide a mechanism for animals to move freely around the forest interior.

Many, like rattans, have barbs and thorns that are used by the plant to attach themselves to their host. They also have an unwelcome habit of hooking themselves into unsuspecting human flesh, so hikers need to be careful walking along the trails. The Rattan is one of the best-known plants in the Malaysian rainforest, since it is commercially harvested to make cane furniture. The Orang Asli people have remarkable skills in removing the prickly barbs of this vine.

Another plant that looks like a vine is the Strangler Fig, whose seeds are deposited by birds which eat the fruit and pass seeds onto branches in the forest canopy. The germinating seeds spread their roots downwards and these encircle the host tree. Eventually the strangler fig is so successful in enveloping the host tree, the latter dies and the fig survives. However, while the host is still alive, the fig looks like a vine.

Forest Fauna

The animal community in the forests of Taman Negara comprises an intriguing variety of life forms. The list of Malaysian fauna is impressive – 200 mammals, over 1,000 butterflies, 600 birds, and over 100 species of both snakes and frogs.

While there are many animals in the park, visitors will probably hear them and locate their tracks more than they will see the creatures themselves. The forests provide natural camouflage for most animals and therefore they are hard to spot. Endangered species like Sumatran Rhinoceros are only seen once in a life-

Rainforest Creatures

While the rainforest is home to many animals, sightings are more difficult than in other habitats. This is due mainly to plant density, tree height and the secretive nature of many species. Animals are attracted to fruiting trees, water, salt licks and grassy open areas. Keen naturalists will seek out these areas as well as the parks hides for the best chance of sighting animals.

time by park rangers, so while such species are mentioned here, don't be frustrated by their elusiveness. Instead, relax in the knowledge that they are there in the park and if you are lucky enough to see one, it really is a moment to treasure for life.

The park hides (*bumbun*) adjoining salt licks are the best place for patient wildlife watchers. (See page 31 for details of hides). Sambar Deer, Barking Deer, Wild Boar and Tapir are often seen around the licks and are best viewed with binoculars.

The following account describes a few of the better known species of animal in the park.

MAMMALS

Some 200 mammal species are known to live in Taman Negara. These range in size from the smallest shrews to the largest elephants. Some are virtually impossible to find while others are guaranteed sightings.

Tapir (*Tapirus indicus*)

Tapirs are one of the strangest rainforest animals, looking like a cross between a pig and a miniature elephant. They are protected in Malaysia but are still keenly sought by foreign zoos. It is thought that this family once had a much larger range, including Europe and North America, but today it is confined to South-East Asia and South America. Adults are about the size of a large pig but black and white in colour. Young tapirs have distinctive pale markings on a dark body. Being nocturnal feeders on young leaves and fruits, they are best seen after dark from one of the park's hides.

Sumatran Rhinoceros (*Dicerorhinus sumatrensis*)

One of the rarest animals on Earth, with just over 120 thought to be still alive in Peninsular Malaysia and Sabah, this is the smallest of the world's five rhinoceros species and has two horns. The horns are composed of hardened hair, and the supposed aphrodisiac powers of this horn and other parts of the animal's anatomy have led to ruthless hunting. This, combined with the widespread destruction of its forest habitat, has brought the rhino ever closer to extinction. The animal is indeed a rare sight, and a visitor to Taman Negara is highly unlikely to see one. This large herbivore needs extensive tracts of undisturbed rainforest, where it often rests during the heat of the day in a mud wallow, shaded spot or ridge top.

Asian Elephant (*Elaphas maximus*).
There are only about 1,000 elephants remaining on Peninsular Malaysia, many of them within Taman Negara. Their numbers in the park have been increased by a translocation programme from other parts of Peninsular Malaysia.

The clearing of lowland forest has meant that the range for these animals is considerably reduced. Elephants are seldom seen, but are more active in rainy weather and, some say, on bright moonlit nights. A nearby herd betrays its presence with low rumbling sounds, the snapping and cracking of branches, and occasional trumpeting. Such herds are sometimes sighted around Bumbun Kumbang and near Kuala Keniam.

Asian Elephants stay within range of areas with access to fresh water, natural salt licks and an ample supply of food. Adult elephants can consume up to 150 kilograms (330 pounds) of vegetation a day. They feed mainly on the growing parts of palms, soft grasses and banana stems and need a large feeding range to survive. As large parcels of land are cleared for plantations the nation's wild elephant population is being reduced to several isolated herds on shrinking islands of forest. Physical boundaries and bottlenecks constrict their movement and suppress opportunities for genetic exchange necessary for their long-term survival.

Seladang, Gaur or Wild Cattle (*Bos gaurus*)
This animal stands almost 2 metres (6 feet) high and can weigh up to 900 kilograms (2,000 pounds). It is the world's largest species of cattle and is distinguished by a ridge

Asian Elephant

that runs from the neck to half way down the back. It is endangered, with only about 600 animals left in Malaysia, though it is distributed in other parts of South-East Asia and India. It grazes in open areas adjoining forests, but prefers to rest in the cooler shaded areas. It also frequents salt licks for valuable nutrients. Mostly black, it has a conspicuous white forehead and 'stockings'.

Sambar or Rusa Deer *(Cervus unicolor)*
This nocturnal deer is the largest in the rainforest, growing to the size of a pony. It is grey-brown in colour and it is more usual to see females and their young than the antlered males, who tend to lead a solitary existence. A few tame individuals can often be seen around the TNR.

Barking Deer *(Muntiacus muntjak)*
This small deer, slightly larger than a goat, is deep orangy-red in colour with dark markings on the head and a patch of white on the rump under the tail. It is mostly seen feeding at dusk and dawn – especially around Bumbun Tabing.

Lesser Mousedeer *(Tragulus javanicus)*
The Mousedeer is a secretive and mostly solitary little creature, the size of a small dog, and brown in colour with a white stripe at the side of the throat. The Greater Mousedeer *(Tragulus napu)* is also found in the park. In Malaysia, the Mousedeer is a well-known animal called a *Kancil*, after which one of Malaysia's national cars is named. There is also a famous Malay folk tale hero called Sang Kancil.

Wild Pig *(Sus scrofa)*
These widespread animals are grey in colour, usually covered in mud, and smaller than domestic pigs. They are often seen in small groups along park trails and heard in the evening grunting around the chalets at the TNR. The wild pig is omnivorous and eats tubers, roots and fruits as well as small animals such as reptiles.

Black Giant Squirrel *(Ratufa bicolor)*
Squirrels belong to the rodentia order of animals so they have similarities with rats and mice. The two species of giant squirrel are usually found by themselves high in trees and the Canopy Walk is a good place to look. Both are about the size of a cat and the black squirrel is predominantly black with white cheeks and underparts.

Cream Giant Squirrel *(Ratufa affinis)*
This species shares the size and characteristics of the black squirrel but is honey-brown in colour.

Prevost's Squirrel *(Callosciurus prevostii)*
Prevost's is the most colourful of the tree squirrels, being mostly black with a chestnut belly and legs and a white stripe along the flank. This squirrel is about 20-25 centimetres (8-10 inches) long.

ABOVE: THE MAGNIFICENT BUT
ELUSIVE TIGER IS SELDOM
ENCOUNTERED BY VISITORS,
THOUGH ITS DISTINCTIVE TRACKS
ARE OCCASIONALLY SPOTTED
ALONG THE FOREST TRAILS.

RIGHT: THE FEMALE SAMBAR DEER,
A FAVOURITE PREY OF TIGERS, IS
MORE OFTEN SEEN THAN THE
MALE. A NUMBER OF TAME INDI-
VIDUALS FREQUENT THE AREA
AROUND TAMAN NEGARA RESORT.

OPPOSITE TOP LEFT: THE WHOOPING CALLS OF THE WHITE-HANDED GIBBON RESONATE THROUGH THE FOREST AT DAWN FROM HIGH IN THE CANOPY.

OPPOSITE TOP RIGHT: THE COLUGO, OR FLYING LEMUR, IS PERFECTLY CAMOU-FLAGED AGAINST FOREST TREE TRUNKS.

OPPOSITE BELOW: ASIAN ELEPHANTS ARE MORE OFTEN HEARD THAN SEEN, THOUGH THERE ARE REGULAR SIGHTINGS AROUND BUMBUN KUMBANG AND KUALA KENIAM.

ABOVE: THE BIZARRE APPEARANCE AND DEEP CALL OF THE RHINOCEROS HORN-BILL MAKE IT ONE OF THE MOST EASILY RECOGNISED FOREST BIRDS.

RIGHT: THE SPECTACULAR DISPLAY OF THE MALE GREAT ARGUS PHEASANT IS USED TO ATTRACT FEMALES.

TOP: AMONGST A WEALTH OF BUTTERFLY SPECIES THE RAJAH BROOK BIRDWING STANDS OUT FOR ITS SIZE, SWOOPING FLIGHT AND DAZZLING COLOURS.

ABOVE: THE RETICULATED PYTHON, THE WORLD'S LONGEST SNAKE, TAKES PREY UP TO THE SIZE OF DEER, BUT IS ELUSIVE AND SELDOM ENCOUNTERED.

LEFT: MANY INSECTS, SUCH AS THE LEAF MANTIS, ARE CUNNINGLY ADAPTED TO LIFE IN THE FOREST.

Flying Lemur or Colugo (*Cynocephalus variegatus*)
The Flying Lemur is not a true lemur since, unlike lemurs, it is not a primate. Neither strictly speaking can it fly, but actually glides from tree to tree using a flying membrane that stretches between its arms and legs. Its amazing camouflage, with grey-brown and off-white patches, resembles the lichen patches found on the trees where it lives. This camouflage and its largely nocturnal lifestyle make it difficult to spot during the day.

PRIMATES

Long-tailed or Crab-eating Macaque (*Macaca fascicularis*)
Chances are, any monkey visitors see in Taman Negara will be a Long-tailed Macaque. This common species has a reddish-brown back, grey front, limbs and whiskers and is often seen along rivers, especially the Tembeling. It is rarely found alone but more normally in large troops of at least ten adults and young.

Dusky Leaf-monkey (*Presbytis obscura*)
Leaf-monkeys, also known as langurs, are distinguished from macaques in that they have longer tails, longer hair and they eat only leaves. This species is dark, with conspicuous white rings around the eyes and mouth that have led to its alternative name of Spectacled Leaf-monkey. They are not that common in Taman Negara but are found along the Jenut Muda Trail and the Kuala Tahan to Kuala Trenggan Trail. Groups may be heard crashing through treetops when disturbed.

Banded Leaf-monkey (*Presbytis melalophos*)
Grey with black face, feet, tail and hands, these monkeys have long tails and crash very loudly through the forest when disturbed. Often seen at dusk around some of the hides, as well as along the Jenut Muda Trail. Frequently calls at night.

White-handed Gibbon (*Hylobates lar*)
Gibbons are the smallest apes and the ones least closely related to Man. They have no tail, but long hands and arms on which they swing through the rainforest canopy from tree to tree at great speed. Gibbons live in family groups that jointly defend a territory in the treetops. They rarely come out of the canopy to feed and therefore are seldom seen, although their ringing calls are frequently heard in the forest early in the morning. The colour of this species varies from black to cream but it always has a pale ring around the face.

Siamang (*Hylobates syndactylus*)
The Siamang is the largest of the gibbons. It is completely black with rather shaggy fur and a bare throat patch that inflates when the animal is calling. Early in the morning a group's 'whooping' calls can boom across the hills and valleys for several kilometres. and are one of the most memorable sounds of the dawn chorus. This call can sometimes be heard high up in the trees along the Canopy Walk. The Siamang's diet consist mainly of leaves, flowers and fruits – especially figs.

Slow Loris (*Nycticebus coucang*)

The Slow Loris is a small nocturnal primate whose large eyes are best sighted on a night walk or spotlighting adventure. As the name suggests, it moves slowly through the forest trees, feeding mainly on insects, small animals, birds and fruit.

CARNIVORES

Malayan Sun Bear or Honey Bear (*Helarctos malayanus*).

With a body length of just over one metre (3 feet), the Malayan Sun Bear is the smallest of the world's seven bears and the only species found in South-East Asia, where its range extends deep into the region. It feeds on fruits, small animals, and the nests of termites and bees. It is very rarely seen and its population is believed to be declining. A typical sign that a Sun Bear has been present are its claw marks on trees that are in fruit or that contain the nests of bees and termites. These animals are generally harmless, but recent reported attacks in other parts of Malaysia suggests some caution if they are encountered. The Sun Bear has poor eyesight and hearing but has an acute sense of smell. It is an able climber, and uses its powerful claws for leverage. Sun bears are more active in daylight. While bears are fully protected under the law they are still threatened by illegal hunting – mostly for spurious medicinal and aphrodisiac markets.

Malayan Tiger (*Panthera tigris corbetti*)

This magnificent animal needs little description. Largest of the forest predators, males can grow up to almost 2.5 metres (8 feet) in length and weigh 150 kilograms (330 pounds). The Tiger is a fully protected species, and there are thought to be no more than 300 left in Malaysia. Like the Panther and the Golden Cat, the Tiger is only found on Peninsular Malaysia and not Borneo. Sadly the Tiger is still illegally hunted, with various parts of the anatomy being used in traditional medicines and as an aphrodisiac. Being rare, elusive and beautifully camouflaged, tigers are

Malayan Tiger

scarcely ever seen by visitors, but fresh tracks in patches of mud and beside streams may reveal their presence.

Black Panther or Leopard *(Panthera pardus)*
The Black Panther is the dark and more common colour phase of the familiar spotted Leopard. It is the second largest cat in Malaysia, and is probably seen even less frequently than the Tiger. Primarily solitary, Black Panthers take a wide range of prey - from deer and wild pigs to birds and even insects. Male Black Panthers weigh up to 33 kilograms (73 pounds) and are about 2 metres (6 feet) in length.

Clouded Leopard *(Neofelis nebulosa)*
Found exclusively in the rainforest, and these days rarely seen because of its rarity and shyness, the Clouded Leopard has endangered status. It feeds on birds, monkeys and squirrels. While it grows to about 1.5 metres (5 feet) in length it only weighs about 15 kilograms (33 pounds). It is mainly nocturnal and lives in trees from which it often leaps on prey below. An exceptionally long tail helps it balance when moving through the branches.

Golden Cat *(Captopuma (Felis) temmincki)*
The Golden Cat grows to about 1.2 metres (4 feet) and weighs some 10 kilograms (22 pounds). Little is known about the ecology of this cat which lives mostly on the ground but also climbs trees if necessary. It feeds on smaller animals such as birds, Mousedeer and lizards.

Leopard Cat *(Prionailurus (Felis) bengalensis)*
The Leopard Cat is similar in size to a domestic cat and is widespread throughout a variety of forest habitats in South-East Asia.

Smooth Otter *(Lutra perspicillata)*
Smooth Otters can often be seen surfacing and diving along the rivers. Adults are about 75 centimetres (30 inches) long. Their close coat of waterproof hair and their webbed feet ideally suit them to their riverine habitat. Otters do not live exclusively in the water and may be seen on riverbanks and in adjoining forests.

Small-clawed Otter *(Amblonyx cinera)*
This species is smaller than the Smooth Otter and has a distinguishing white throat. It is seen more in the smaller tributaries of the Tembeling, especially Sungai Tahan, rather than the main river.

Common Palm Civet *(Paradoxurus hermaphroditus)*
Civets are cat-like animals growing to about a metre (a yard) in length and commonly found in Malaysian forests. They have a long tail, a pointed muzzle and alternating dark and light grey stripes. Of several species in the park, this is the most frequently encountered. It feeds on a variety of plant and animal matter.

BIRDS

638 bird species within 78 bird families have been recorded in Peninsular Malaysia. Of these, 426 species are classified as residents, with the remaining 212 species being made up of migrants, winter visitors or vagrants. Diverse bird habitats include montane forest, lowland forest – of which Taman Negara is the most significant in the region – coasts and open habitats, such as rice fields and coconut plantations.

Of all these species, over 300 have been recorded in Taman Negara, a number unmatched by any other wildlife area in the region. Some real rarities have been recorded here, including a number of endangered species such as Storm's Stork (*Ciconia stormi*), Malay Peacock Pheasant (*Polyplectron malacensis*) and the Green Imperial Pigeon (*Ducula aenea*). Among the park's other more noted species are the Lesser Fish-eagle *(Ichthyophaga nana)*, the Green-billed Malcoha (*Phaenicophaeus tristis)* and the White-crowned Hornbill (*Aceros comatus*). Some species have very localised habitats, such as swiftlets which are only found in the limestone caves of the park, where they use echo location to navigate through their dark environment.

As well as a good pair of binoculars, a notebook, some sturdy walking boots and warm waterproof clothing, a good field guide is indispensable. Serious birders should take a copy of the fully illustrated and comprehensive *Identification Guide to the Birds of South-East Asia* (Craig Robson, New Holland). A lighter, easier-to-carry guide to many of the park's species is *A Photographic Guide to the Birds of Peninsular Malaysia and Singapore* (G.W.H. Davison and Chew Yen Fook, New Holland).

The following account describes a few of the better known bird species in the park, including some of those most likely to be encountered by the visitor.

Hornbills

Hornbills are the crowning glory of the rainforest canopy. These large majestic birds have striking plumage, long tails and the distinctive horn-shaped bill that gives them their name. Nine species of hornbill have been recorded in the park: Rhinoceros (*Buceros rhinoceros*), Black (*Anthracoceros malayanus*), Great (*Buceros bicornis*), Helmeted (*Buceros vigil*), Wrinkled (*Aceros corrugatus*), Oriental Pied (*Anthracoceros albiroftris*), Wreathed (*Aceros undulatus*), White-crowned (*Aceros comatus*) and Bushy-crested Hornbill (*Anorrhinus galeritus*).

All species of hornbill share the same unusual nesting behaviour, with females settling into a hole in a tree, and walling themselves in with their own droppings. The male helps by adding pieces of wood and dollops of mud from the outside. A narrow opening is left for the male to feed his mate and young chick. When the young hornbill is ready to learn to fly, the wall of mud is knocked away.

Hornbills feed on fruits and small animals. The strong pair bonding keeps many hornbill partners together for years. Hornbills often frequent riverine forest, where it is not unusual to see several pairs in the one tree or swooping noisily overhead.

The **Rhinoceros Hornbill** measures 1.3 metres (4 foot) from head to tail. It has a yellow and red *casque*, and a distinctive white tail with a single black band. Rhinoceros Hornbills are often seen flying overhead while making loud, deep calls.

The **Helmeted Hornbill** has a 75 centimetre (3 foot) long tail. Its bill, neck and

Hornbills are classic birds of the lowland rainforest and their huge bills and casques (enlargement of the upper part of the bill) make them particularly distinctive, even to the novice birdwatcher. Their large size, varying from the Pied Hornbill at 70 cm (30 in) to the magnificent Helmeted Hornbill at 125 cm (50 in) also makes them relatively easy to spot. Gregarious, noisy birds, they are often to be found feasting on fruiting trees or catching a variety of large-winged insects.

The nine species to be found in Taman Negara, in ascending order of size, are as follows:

Pied Hornbill	Bushy-crested Hornbill	Great Hornbill
Black Hornbill	White-crowned Hornbill	Rhinoceros Hornbill
Wrinkled Hornbill	Wreathed Hornbill	Helmeted Hornbill

casque are dark red. Unlike other hornbills, the *casque* is solid and resembles ivory. This bird's bizaare call consists of a series of loud 'hoops' which eventually develop into hysterical laughter. In territorial displays, a loud knocking sound is made when the birds bang their *casque* against trees or when competing birds bang their casques together.

The commonly seen **Black Hornbill** and **Pied Hornbill** are recognisable by their smaller size. **The Black Hornbill** is almost all black and makes a noisy retching call, while the **Pied Hornbill** has a black and white pattern on its bill and *casque*.

The **Wreathed Hornbill** is usually recognisable by the swooshing of its wingbeat. It sports a bright yellow pouch on its throat and has a high-pitched call. The **Wrinkled Hornbill** is very similar, but its neck pouch is white or blue.

Bushy-crested Hornbills tend to occur in family groups of about ten, and are usually recognised by their squeaky laughter and the fluttering of their wings as they move among the trees. Their heads are adorned with fluffy white feathers.

White-breasted Waterhen (*Amaurornis phoenicurus*)

Known in Malaysia as the *Ruak Ruak* after its call, this species is common around the ponds and salt licks of the park. The bird often leaves this habitat and turns up in many places away from water. It is omnivorous and protected under the law except during the months of May-August when it can be legally hunted for food (except in Taman Negara where all wildlife is protected).

Red Jungle-fowl (*Gallus gallus*)

This species is thought to be the ancestor of the domestic chicken, and it is easy to see why. The male looks like its domestic counterpart but is slimmer, with grey legs and large white ear and rump patches. The female is brown with dark brown streaks. They are a common sight around salt licks, hides and waterholes.

Green-winged Pigeon or Emerald Dove (Chalcophaps indica)
One of the more common pigeons in the park, this species is is often flushed from trails and appears largely green with two white bars on the lower back.

Little Green Pigeon (Treron olax)
Another common pigeon, usually seen in pairs or flocks feeding on fig fruits at altitudes below 1,100 metres (3,600 feet). This species is distinguished by its small size. Male and female both have a similar grey head and green breast. Males also have an orange breast band and maroon wings, while females have a pale throat.

Gold-whiskered Barbet (Megaalaima zeylanica)
Barbets are small but strident hole-nesting forest birds, their loud and repetitive calls being a characteristic sound of the upper canopy. This species is one of the more common, and is easily identified by its oval yellow cheek patch and long, low trilling call.

Yellow-crowned Barbet (Megalaima henrici)
Another common barbet species, with a distinctive yellow forecrown and eyebrow, a blue throat and an endlessly repeated tok tok tok call uttered from high in the canopy.

Straw-headed Bulbul (Pynonotus zeylanicus)
Of the many species of bulbul found in the park this is ceratinly the most frequently seen. It is the largest of the bulbuls, with a distinctive orange head. Its rich, melodious bubbling calls are always to be heard alongside river banks as pairs duet in chorus, especially in the early morning.

Common or White-rumped Shama (Copsychus malabaricus)
The Shama is found singly or in pairs in the lower canopy of lowland forest where it constantly flits about in the understorey. Here it builds its nest in tree holes, using twigs, dried leaves and grasses. Its head and back are glossy black and it has a rust red underside. Shamas, like bulbusl, are popular songsters.

Grey-headed Fish-eagle (Ichthyophaga ichthyaetus)
These birds of prey, with their hooked bills and talons, can be seen along the more open riverbanks, such as on the boat journey from Tembeling to Kuala Tahan, and on some of the rocks near smaller rapids in the park. Being near the top of the food chain they feed on various animals, but in particular on fish. Although rare in other parts of the country this magnificent species is not uncommon in the park.

Lesser Fish-eagle (Ichthyophaga nana)
This species is smaller than the last, with a darker tail. It is also found along the park's rivers, particularly the SungainTahan, but is easily disturbed by boats traffic.

White-breasted Kingfisher (Halcyon smyrnensis)
This is the most common of the 15 kingfisher species found in Malaysia. Kingfishers in

general are characteristically colourful birds, with a large head and bill, short legs and a short tail. They are hole-nesters and have feet specially adapted to accommodate this lifestyle. Most species are found close to water as fish constitute the main part of their diet. In Taman Negara they are usually seen flying low and fast along riverbanks or perching on low-lying branches just above the water. They are mostly solitary hunters. The White-breasted has a bright blue back and wings, brown underparts, a white throat and upper breast. and red bill and legs. It feeds upon riverbank creatures such as lizards, rodents and insects as well as fish.

Lesser Fish-eagle

Stork-billed Kingfisher (*Pelargopsis capensis*)
Unlike the White-breasted Kingfisher, the Stork-billed is commonly seen with a mate along riverbanks in Taman Negara. It is the largest of the Malaysian kingfishers and has a bright red bill with a black tip, a dull greyish brown head, bright yellow collar and a shiny blue back. Its feeding habits are similar to the White-breasted Kingfisher.

Masked Finfoot (*Heliopais personata*)
This unusual duck-like, greyish-brown bird with a yellow and orange bill tends to skulk under dark overhung banks. It is found along the Sungai Tahan from February to June. Being rare throughout its range, it is much sought after by birdwatchers.

Garnet Pitta (*Pitta granatina*)
This beautiful ground-dwelling bird is an inhabitant of the forest floor, especially in moist, well-shaded locations. It has a distinct, quavering, near monotone whistle.

Scarlet-rumped Trogon (*Harpactes duvauceli*)
Like all trogons, this species has brilliant plumage (black head and scarlet rump and breast) but is often seen in poor light sitting quietly in the lower canopy.

Black and Red Broadbill (*Cymbirhynchus macrorhynchos*)
There are a number of broadbills in the forest. This bright-coloured species is commonly seen beside water where it builds an untidy globular nest from a branch overhanging the river. In the park, it is often found around Lata Berkoh.

Raffles Malcoha (*Phaenicophaeus chlorophaeus*)
Malcohas are members of the cuckoo family that tend to spend their time scrambling around in dense foliage. They are frequently seen in pairs, the male Raffles Malcoha with its chestnut underparts and blackish tail is easier to spot than the female.

Greater Coucal (*Centropus sinensis*)
These large black birds with chestnut wings are fairly common in the riverine forests. They are often observed as they cross the rivers with a few slow wing beats followed by a long glide into dense foliage.

Mountain Peacock Pheasant (*Polyplectron inopinatum*)
There are eight pheasant species in Malaysia and they have a common characteristic of living on the ground rather than in trees. This bird is only found in Peninsular Malaysia in mountain forests between 900 and 2,200 metres (3,000 and 7,000 feet). It has largely chestnut upperparts.

Great Argus Pheasant (*Argusianus argus*)
This very large bird is found in forests at up to 900 metres (3,000 feet). The males mate with more than one female and use loud calls and courtship displays of their long tails and ornamental feathers to attract females. Both sexes are solitary and the female normally incubates the eggs without any male assistance.

Crested Fireback Pheasant (*Lophura ignita*)
Both males and female of this colourful species have an erect crest but the male has a more spectacular plumage of dark bluish violet with an orange patch on the back. The female is an overall brown colour with black and white scale-like feathers on the belly, throat and breast. They are a reasonably common sight along riverside trails in the park. Males attract females by whirring their wings.

Crested Argus Pheasant
(*Rheinardia ocellata*)
This large pheasant is mostly dark brownish, spotted with white and with an enormous tail. In Malaysia it is only found on a few mountains in Taman Negara such as Rabung, Tahan, Gagau and Mandi Angin. It lives at up to and around 900 metres (3,000 feet) on Gunung Tahan.

Black and Red Broadbill

Blue-throated Bee-Eater (*Merops viridis*)
Bee-eaters are bright coloured, active birds. This species is often seen on the river trip from Tembeling to Kuala Tahan as it swoops to catch insects on the wing (not only bees!). In the evening groups gather over the river *en route* to their overnight roost.

REPTILES AND AMPHIBIANS
There are many snakes, lizards, frogs and turtles found in Malaysia and the park. They inlcude some extraordinary creatures such as draco lizards that can glide from tree to tree in search of prey, and the Reticulated Python *(Python reticulatus)* – the world's longest snake – which can suffocate animals as large as deer in its coils.

Fortunately, most of the 140 species of land snakes are non-venomous. The 17 venomous species in Malaysia include the King Cobra *(Ophiophagus hannah)* whose venom will usually prove fatal. However, the Pit Viper is responsible for more serious bites, as it is often found around where people live and work. Its triangular shaped head is a good identifying feature. Like all vipers, it has a heat sensing mechanism that helps it locate warm-blooded organisms in the dark. It should be emphasised that all snakes, including the potentially dangerous ones, are very wary of people, and are seldom encountered on the trail.

There are almost 100 species of lizard found on Peninsular Malaysia including families such as geckos and skinks. Many will be well camouflaged – even a 2 metre (6 feet) long Water Monitor – but most tend to sun themselves on rocks or open sunny ground where there is a break in the canopy, providing an opportunity to spot them.

Taman Negara is also home to several non-marine turtles, tortoises and terrapins, as well as a host of frogs and other amphibians. Two of the more commonly encountered reptiles are:

Water Monitor Lizard **(**Varanus salvator**)**
This shy and harmless scavenger appears more dangerous than it looks. It can grow up to two metres (six feet) and is quite common in open areas and beside rivers where it usually suns itself. Sit quietly in Bumbun Tahan and chances are one will appear on the grassed area below the hide. Monitor lizards use their red forked tongue to sense their environment. This tongue is completely harmless. If disturbed the lizard can move very quickly and noisily to seek refuge.

Racer Snakes
The Cave Racer Snake *(Elaphe taeniura)* inhabits the park's caves where it feeds on frogs, rodents and bats. Up to 2.5 metres (8 feet) in length, this handsome and fast-moving snake is greenish-yellow and darker towards the last third of its body

FISHES
The rivers of the park support healthy freshwater fish populations. Fishing is a popular recreational activity in most parts of the park but especially the Kuala Koh and Terengganu access points. See page 43 for details of fishing sites, tackle and most popular species.

MICRO FAUNA

Visitors to the rainforest can expect to see many more insects and other small organisms than larger animals. For the patient and observant visitor, this micro world offers a mini safari of fascinating richness and diversity. And some of the micro fauna is not even all that 'micro', with species of the giant millipede reaching lengths of 25 centimetres (10 inches).

In many parts of the forest, particularly on the leaf litter of the forest floor, visitors can see earthworms, spiders, leeches, ticks, mites, centipedes, ants and scorpions. There are too many species (known and unknown) for scientists to record – such is the wealth and mystery of the tropical rainforest.

Spiders

In Taman Negara, spiders can be found in most habitats, including the limestone caves.

Golden Orb Web Spiders are common just off many of the trails. This species is the most commonly encountered of all the large spiders in Malaysia. The black and gold spider seen in the web is the female, who dwarfs the miniscule male. The web is very strong and can reportedly catch large insects and even small birds.

Insects

Insects are the most numerous living organisms on Earth with over 1 million known species and perhaps millions more yet to be identified. Insects include butterflies, moths, bees, dragonflies, damselflies, mosquitoes, flies, beetles and cockroaches.

There are over 1,000 butterflies in Malaysia but one of the more beautiful is the enormous black, lime green and red Rajah Brooke's Birdwing .

Among the ant species in Malaysia there are about 100 where the ant has a constant association with a specific plant species to the mutual benefit of both plants and animals.

Termites play an integral role in maintaining the fertility of the thin rainforest topsoil. They not only aerate the soil but also move large quantities of decaying humus to lower soil levels. Their role in the carbon and nutrient cycles is crucial.

Leeches

The leech is a much maligned organism whose reputation is far worse than its bite. Leeches can go for months between 'sucks' or feeds. They impart an anticoagulant while feeding, so that the

Rajah Brooke's Birdwing

blood continues to flow even after the leech has dropped off. Leeches lurk about waiting for some 'sucker' to come along and attach themselves, feed, expanding up to three times their body size, and then drop off. Leech bites are a little painful and itchy while they heal. The important thing is to scrape off the leech and arrest the blood flow by compression or using cold water.

Scorpions, Millipedes and Centipedes

Millipedes are not poisonous, while scorpions and centipedes can inflict poisonous but not deadly stings. Malaysia's most common millipede is the bright red *Trigoniulus lumbricinus* which can measure up to 5 centimetres (2 inches). As a defence mechanism, it rolls into a ball when there is perceived danger.

FOREST FLORA

The forests of Taman Negara are dominated by the sheer number and variety of plant species. While it is easy to see the large plants, visitors should also take some time out to look at things on a micro level. For example, examining the bark of one of the larger trees will reveal a wealth of miniature life such as lichen, moss, fungi and liverworts. Some of this is not actually plant life or flora in that some plants do not produce their own food but rather live on dead organic matter (e.g. fungi).

Leech movements

By 'looping', a leech can move with surprising speed. It stretches its head forward as far as it will go and then brings the tail up to meet it by bending the body into a great loop.

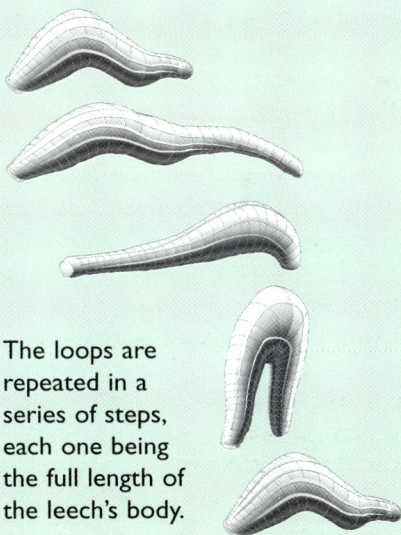

The loops are repeated in a series of steps, each one being the full length of the leech's body.

Palms

Palms are found in most habitats in Malaysia, but especially the lowland forests. Palms are important economically as well as ecologically. In Malaysia, coconuts, rattans and the imported African oil palm generate significant economic returns for the country. At a local level villagers use many palms for food, baskets, housing, furniture, medicines, hunting equipment, binding and fish traps.

Rattans are commonly found in rainforests with 200 species in the country, 20 of which are used commercially. Most are climbers and can grow to considerable heights, with many reaching the forest canopy. Harvesting rattan in the wild for sale is a skill best known to the Orang Asli. The spines of the rattan palm are particularly strong and assist the plant to 'climb' upwards to the canopy. Visitors to Taman Negara need to pay close attention to these spines, and those of other plants, as they easily rip through human flesh.

Mosses, Liverworts and Hornworts

These terrestrial plants are collectively known as bryophytes, and after the flowering plants, they are the most diverse plant group in Malaysia. They do not have true roots but rather root-like structures called rhizoids that anchor them to a host and enable them to obtain water. As they like moist and protected areas bryophytes are more common in the higher altitude montane forests of Taman Negara.

The blue-green club moss found in the understorey along the trail to the Canopy Walk is an exception. This moss is particularly spectacular because of its unique colour and carpet-like expanse in some areas.

Ferns

Ferns are non-flowering plants that are common in the understorey throughout the lowland and montane forests of Taman Negara. They reproduce through minute spores found in spore cases on the plants. There are many species of ferns with over 500 being recorded in Peninsular Malaysia. There are several forms of fern: those that grow in the rainforest soil, climbing ferns, creepers and even epiphytic ferns. On Gunung Tahan, epiphytic ferns cover the trunks and branches of the dwarfed trees. One such fern, *Lecanopteris carnosa,* is an interesting 'ant fern'. A symbiotic relationship occurs in that the plant provides shelter and food for the ants while the ants provide minerals and nitrogen for the fern.

Fungi

Fungi are essential to the rainforest ecosystem as they help break down decaying vegetation into humus that becomes the nutrient for plant species. The relationship between fungi and plants can be quite complex with some orchid seeds, for example, only germinating in the presence of specific fungi. Some fungi (mycorrhizal fungi), extend from plant roots and transfer nutrient to plants.

There are also luminescent fungi in Taman Negara and a good place to see them is just beyond the TNR on the Canopy Walk. Just walk 50 metres (50 yards) into the forest, turn off your torch and look carefully for the tiny bluish lights near the ground.

Lichens

Lichens are very complex organisms that take three forms; foliose, crustose and fruticose. One of the most common forms in Taman Negara looks like an iridescent paint that has been sprayed on moist tree trunks, rocks and building surfaces. Others look like flaky paint or hair – the latter are commonly called 'Old Man's Beard'.

Gingers

One of the more interesting groups of plants are the gingers, of which 288 species are located in Malaysia. They typically occur in lowland forests up to an altitude of 500 metres (1,600 feet). and many have spectacular flowers.

Parasites

In Malaysia there are several plants that do not photosynthesise and therefore do not manufacture their own food. *Rafflesia,* the world's largest flower, is one such parasitic plant. The 15 species of *Rafflesia* are only found in South-East Asia, with three occurring in Peninsular Malaysia.

Orchids

There are over 850 orchid species in Peninsular Malaysia with most occurring where the light intensity is good. The forest floors of Taman Negara are, therefore, not good areas to see orchids

Supporting plants

A single giant forest tree plays host to dozens of species of orchids, mosses and ferns. These epiphytic plants have no connection with the ground, but collect their water and nutrients from the damp recesses into which their roots grow.
Creepers and strangler figs also use the tree as a physical support from which to reach the light above and the soil below.

though they do grow in the more open exposed areas. Most are epiphytic so around tree trunks and rock surfaces are good areas to start looking.

FOREST PEOPLE

Orang Asli – The Batek (or Bateq)

While many Orang Asli people have settled in permanent communities near the park, there are still Batek people living a semi-traditional life in Taman Negara. The Batek people are one of the Negrito tribes and have similarities to people from the Andaman Islands, the Philippines, Indonesia and New Guinea. They are true nomads and are classified by some anthropologists as pygmies due to their short stature.

There are several theories on the harmonious relationship between the Orang Asli people and their habitat. One group of anthropologists suggests that hunters and gatherers could not have occupied tropical rainforests independently without access to sedentary agricultural populations with whom they would have traded goods. This theory presupposes that rainforests are not easy environments for humans to survive in.

The survival of the Orang Asli in the rainforest was partly dependent upon using a series of limestone caves for shelter. In 1985 charcoal drawings were discovered in Gua Batu Luas in Taman Negara and attributed to the ancestors of the Batek people. While they only date from 1920, anthropologists have speculated that the traditions of cave painting amongst these people is much older. The motifs found in the cave include mountain scenery that is most likely Gunung Tahan.

Today, about 500 Orang Asli live in the park at any one time. It is possible to visit their communities as long as a recognised guide accompanies you. There isn't a great deal to see as the Orang Asli live a very simple hunter-gatherer lifestyle. The accommodation is extremely simple, but for visitors who want to learn about these people it is possible to stay with them and accompany them on their daily activities such as forays into the forest in search of food.

The camp usually comprises 10 to 30 family members living in temporary shelters made from natural vegetation. There is a slightly raised sleeping platform for protection from insects and an open hearth for cooking and heat. The settlements are located near rivers and the structures are not sturdy as they are only needed for a few months before the community moves on.

Contact with the outside is limited, although the Batek sell some forest products like rattan, which they are adept at collecting. They also collect and eat many forest fruits and plants such as durian, cempedak, mangosteen, rambutan and petai, and may sell any excess. Many natural products are used in their everyday life.

Orang Asli communities move according to seasonal food requirements or when an area is nearly exhausted of food. It is not part of their character to destroy an area, and they move on before the resources are depleted. The forest is their 'supermarket' and therefore valued and – as the home of their ancestors – respected.

The men hunt and share the spoils while the women fish and collect forest fruits and vegetables. The Orang Asli are renowned for their hunting prowess. The Batek believe animals living above the ground are clean so they hunt those living in trees such as birds, squirrels and monkeys. Originally the Orang Asli used bows and arrows but early this century they converted to blowpipes. Today, they still use 1.5metre (5 foot) bamboo blowpipes and poisonous darts to hunt on a daily basis. Darts are dipped in the poisonous sap of the Ipoh Tree (*Antaris toxicaria*).

Traps and nets are occasionally used to snare small game. Meals are supplemented with fish, tortoises, jungle fruits and yams from the forest and products like rice bought from outside. Traditionally most food was cooked in bamboo, grilled or boiled although now metal pots supplement this.

Usually visitors to any Orang Asli community pay their guide for all travel arrangements and the community receives some of the money. While offering a gift is appreciated, visitors need to be careful about the type of gift. For example sweets, cigarettes and junkfood are inappropriate while rice and other staples are appreciated.

Conservation

Taman Negara is a national park that has been established to preserve the flora and fauna for the benefit and appreciation of today's and tomorrow's generations. Tourism is merely one important aspect of the park and unless managed and controlled, could lead to destruction of the very elements that tourists come to see. Sustainable or responsible tourism involves delicate management of people and natural resources so that tourism and the natural resource are both perpetuated.

All visitors have a special responsibility to minimise their impact upon the park while they are visiting. The park managers have the important task of managing, educating and guiding visitors while in the park. Educating visitors means that more ambassadors for Taman Negara and the Malaysian rainforest spread these important conservation messages. For more information about what you can do to protect the park, see *Protecting the Park* (page 33).

Trails

Taman Negara offers a variety of trails to suit all visitors, from short walks of an hour or two, to more serious treks of several days Apart from the rivers, walking is the the best mode of travel throughout the park and the best way to appreciate its wonders. The trails are of varying difficulty but there is something for most mobile people who have some degree of fitness and a sense of adventure. Since many trails have river connections, there is often an option of a quicker and more relaxing return journey.

The trails described mostly start at or near the Kuala Tahan entrance to the park although there is some information on the less frequented trails around Kuala Koh, Merapoh and from the Terengganu side. Each trail has its own map (for which you should refer to the map legend on the inside cover) and each section includes a trek planner box.

Trail times vary, depending upon the interests of each walker, distractions along the way, the weather and individual stamina. The times given here represent how long it should take a reasonably fit person to make the distance without too much stopping.

TRAIL TIPS

To make the most of any walk in the forest it helps to be prepared. While prior jungle-trekking experience can be an advantage for walks that involve overnight stays in the forest, a few simple tips can enhance the experience of the first-time visitor.

● Walking in the humid tropics can be energy-sapping. Bring plenty of drinking water, even on short trails.
● The best time to be on the trails is at dusk or dawn when animals are most active and the temperature is cooler.
● While walking, be alert for the small things as well as the large. Big animals seldom appear, but the tiny details of plant or insect life are always there.
● A guided night walk is most rewarding after having done it by day to fully appreciate the difference. Experienced guides will often spot even the tiniest insect from afar. Bring a torch, and look out for spider's eyes and glowing luminescent fungi.
● Pit toilets are provided at some campsites but elsewhere walkers must use their discretion. Do not use streams, since this can pollute them.
● All rubbish that cannot be completely burnt must be returned to Kuala Tahan. Returning Gunung Tahan walkers must account for their rubbish with the rangers.
● For trails to the best fishing locations, refer to **Activities and Adventure – Fishing** (page 43).
● Unfortunately, difficult terrain makes most trails unsuitable for the physically handicapped.

1 Trails around Kuala Tahan

There are many trails through the Pahang side of the park and, unless otherwise stated, all those described here start from Park HQ at Kuala Tahan. The Canopy Walk Trail is the most walked and certainly a must for all visitors.

TRAILS AROUND KUALA TAHAN: 1a – 1g

Start:	Park HQ at Kuala Tahan.
Finish:	Park HQ at Kuala Tahan.
Distance:	From 1 km (1/2 mile) to 18 km (11 miles).
Duration:	From 1 hour to 1 day
Best time:	February or March, but worth a visit any time of the year.
Conditions:	Lower altitudes: rainforest and rivers. Higher altitudes: hillsides and ridges.
Fitness:	Moderate fitness preferable for longer walks.
Equipment:	Good walking shoes and raincape, leech socks, insect repellent, binoculars and camera.

Trail planner

ABOVE: WALKERS IN THE FOREST SHOULD ALWAYS KEEP AN EYE ON THE CANOPY WHERE PRIMATES, BIRDS AND OTHER ARBOREAL CREATURES MAY BE SPOTTED.

ABOVE RIGHT: BUTTRESS ROOTS PROVIDE SUPPORT FOR RAINFOREST TREES, WHILST ENABLING THEM TO OBTAIN NUTRIENTS FROM THE SHALLOW LEACHED SOILS.

RIGHT: TAMAN NEGARA HAS A WIDE NETWORK OF TRAILS, RANGING FROM SHORT STROLLS AROUND CAMP HEADQUARTERS TO MORE ARDUOUS TREKS OF SEVERAL DAYS. ALL ARE CLEARLY MARKED AND SIGNPOSTED.

ABOVE: THE CANOPY WALKWAY, SUSPENDED 40 METRES (140 FEET) ABOVE THE GROUND, IS A POPULAR ATTRACTION AND ALLOWS VISITORS TO EXPERIENCE THE RAINFOREST ECOSYSTEM FROM A UNIQUE PERSPECTIVE.

LEFT: THE CREAM GIANT SQUIRREL, THE SIZE OF A CAT, SELDOM DESCENDS TO THE GROUND AND CAN OFTEN BE SPOTTED FROM THE CANOPY WALKWAY.

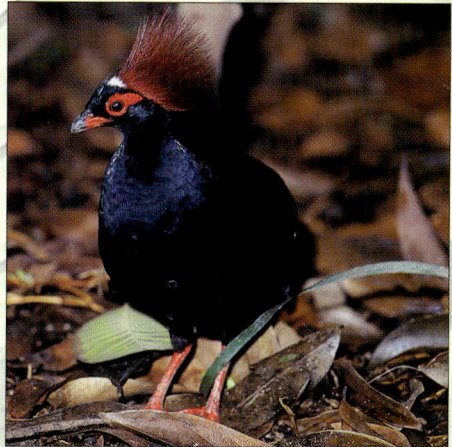

TOP: THE WATER MONITOR LIZARD IS OFTEN SEEN IN OPEN AREAS AROUND THE CAMPS AND HIDES.

ABOVE LEFT: MANY SPECIES OF GINGER ARE FOUND ON THE FOREST FLOOR.

ABOVE RIGHT: QUIET WALKERS MAY MEET CRESTED WOOD PARTRIDGES ALONG THE TRAILS.

RIGHT: PALMS SUCH AS THE WEDGE FAN THRIVE IN THE LOWLAND FOREST ALONG WATER COURSES.

OCCASIONAL GAPS IN THE FOREST AFFORD GLIMPSES OF THE BROAD AND WINDING TEMBELING RIVER.

1a Canopy Walk

This is a relatively easy 3.6 kilometre (2 ¼ mile) return walk through lowland dipterocarp forest. At the end, the world's longest canopy walkway is suspended 40 metres (130 feet) above the ground and provides a bird's eye view into the tall trees of the forest canopy. The 450 metre (500 yard) walkway is made from timber and suspended wire rope and while it sways a bit as people walk, it is quite safe. As a safety precaution, numbers are restricted at any one time and there are several viewing platforms around sturdy trunks of emergent *tualang* trees. The walkway was originally developed for research purposes and while some of this still continues, it is now mainly the domain of inquisitive tourists keen for a slice of adventure and the opportunity to see the rainforest from a unique perspective.

In many ways, the canopy is a different habitat from that at ground level and the plants and animals that live here are not always found in other parts of the rainforest. Squirrels, birds, monkeys and the occasional gibbon may be seen. Look out for orchids and other flowering plants as well.

First time visitors should engage a park guide to interpret the rainforest for them along this trail as it will make subsequent walks more meaningful. The TNR provides guides and the rates are clearly stated at the reception. The trail is however, well marked for those who want to walk independently of a guide.

Just beyond the TNR the understorey is lined with an iridescent blue-green club moss. Along the trail you will notice huge clumps of bamboo – one of the world's tallest grasses – rattan and buttress roots of huge trees.

The Canopy Walk is open from 1100-1445 Saturday to Thursday and 0900-1200 on Friday. Rangers stationed here sell cool drinks and collect fees.

An alternative to the return walk to Park HQ is to hire a boat from the nearby jetty for a five minute trip back.

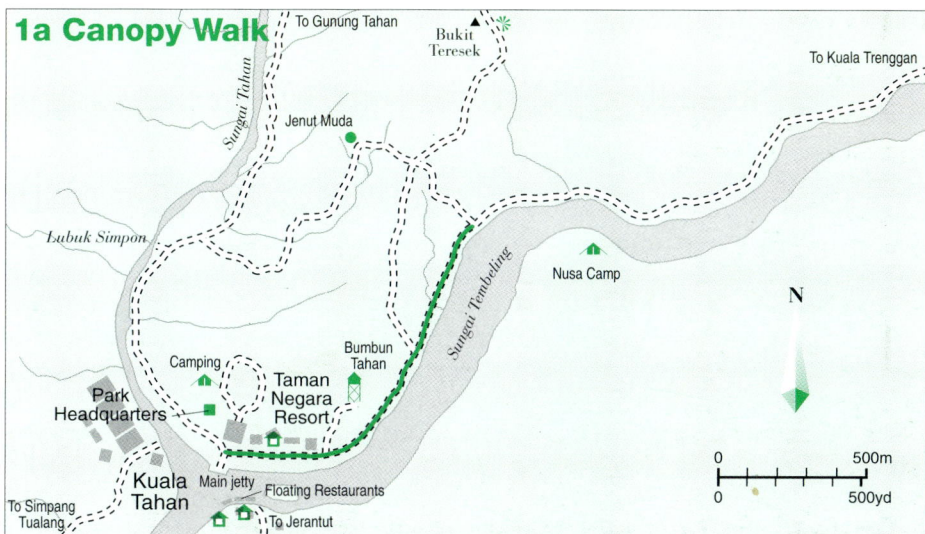

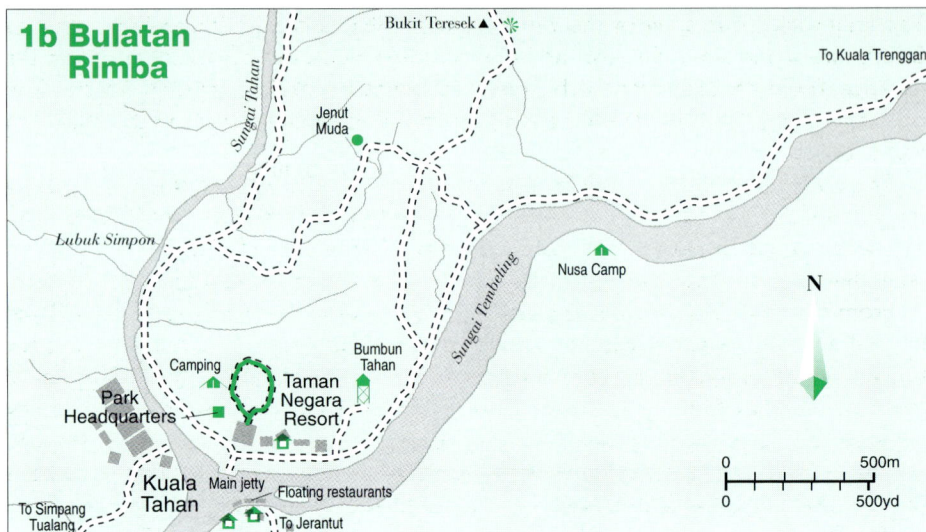

1b Bulatan Rimba

This is a loop trail, less than a kilometre (about half a mile) long, that starts from the back of the TNR. The trail is steep in places, but should be within the capability of most able visitors and only takes about one hour to complete.

Bulatan Rimba offers a wonderful introduction to the forest. It is a good and accessible trail through lowland dipterocarp rainforest. In an anti-clockwise direction, the trail initially follows the sloping sides of a small valley to its head, then drops sharply into a streambed, and finally winds its way back up the ridge. The trail exhibits many classic rainforest features such as epiphytes, lianas and buttress roots. Look out for animal tracks in any muddy patch along the way.

1c Bukit Teresek

At 334 metres (1,096 feet) above sea level, Bukit Teresek is just 1.7 kilometres (1 mile) from Park HQ, with much of the journey up a steep ridge. The popular journey to the summit and back takes about two hours and offers rewarding views of the Sungai Tembeling and Gunung Tahan in the far distance. The trail, like the Canopy Walk Trail, is one of the most accessible from Kuala Tahan. It offers a good introduction to the highlights of the rainforest as well as the more distant views.

The initial part of the trail is the same as the Canopy Walk Trail, running adjacent to the flat riverbank for about 400 metres (440 yards). It then climbs steeply up onto the ridge of Bukit Teresek where there are two look-out points, one at either end of the ridge.

The flat part of the trail at the beginning passes through patches of tall forest and secondary forest not far from the river. Birds representative of these habitats can be found here, and this is considered one of the best bird watching areas in the park, despite the regular flow of trekkers heading to the Canopy Walk.

The long melodious song of the White-rumped Shama can be heard, Straw-headed Bulbuls are found along the river and the Greater Coucal can be heard, well off in the distance. There are also drongos, babblers, malcohas, hornbills and woodpeckers. The open areas near Jenut Muda offer good opportunities to find pittas and the Malaysian Rail Babbler.

The going becomes more difficult as the trail winds its way up the ridge, passing through impressive stands of tall trees. The exposed roots of the emergents make walking more difficult and one needs to keep a steady footing. Giant Squirrels may be seen up in the trees, and White-handed Gibbons can often be heard hooting in the distance.

From the first look-out a small section of the Sungai Tembeling can be seen, and beyond are the forested hills on the other side of the river and outside the park boundary. The semi-rounded boulders at the look-out are sandstone and typical of much of the rock found in the park. From here the rounded crowns of the canopy trees can be viewed from above. Rising above the canopy are the solitary emergents.

The second look-out, ten minutes further on, provides a spectacular view of the high mountains in the centre of Taman Negara and the Sungai Tahan below.

If the weather is clear, Gunung Tahan, to the left at 2,187 metres (7,176 feet) is the highest peak visible. From the look-out the flat profile of the mountain is deceptive and makes Gunung Tahan look lower than the surrounding peaks.

Straight ahead from the look-out is the Upper Tahan Valley, and on the horizon is the conical peak of Gunung Perlis at 1,280 metres (5,000 feet).

Walkers may retrace their steps to Kuala Tahan or return via a path leading down to the left from the second lookout. This steep path winds down to Sungai Tahan, and may be difficult in wet weather. The hillside is covered in tall forest, with many palm species including rattan vines. This path passes by Jenut Muda, an area probably rich in mineral salts that attracts animals. Take time to approach the area quietly and ani-

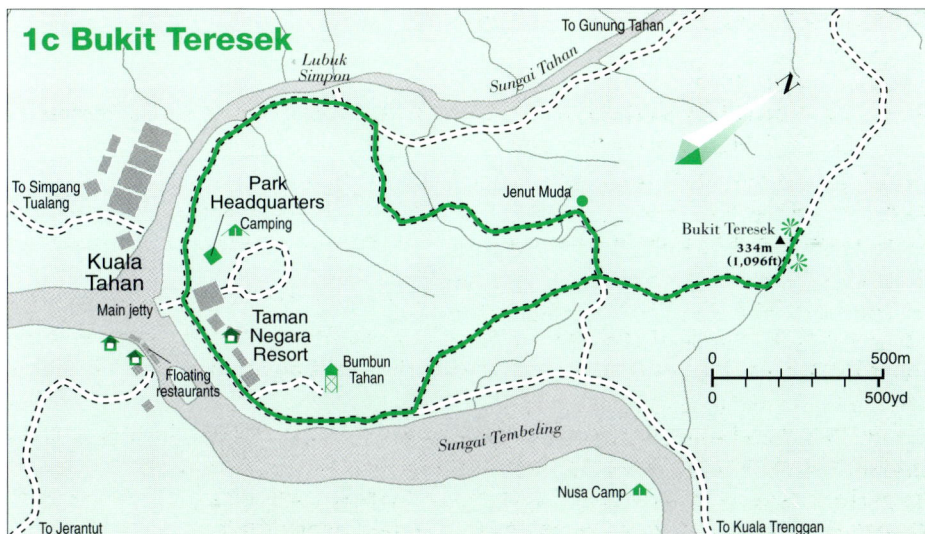

1c Bukit Teresek

mals may be spotted. Look carefully for animal tracks in the soft mud. This route takes a little over an hour from the summit of Butik Teresek, with the final path to Park HQ running parallel to Sungai Tahan.

Another trail leads down to Sungai Tahan and from the river on to Bumbun Tabing and Lata Berkoh.

1d Jenut Muda

While the presence of mineral salts in the soil around Jenut Muda has yet to be confirmed, pigs, deer, and occasionally Tapir visit these two muddy pools at the head of a small gully. Tracks in the soft ground give an indication of

Masked Finfoot

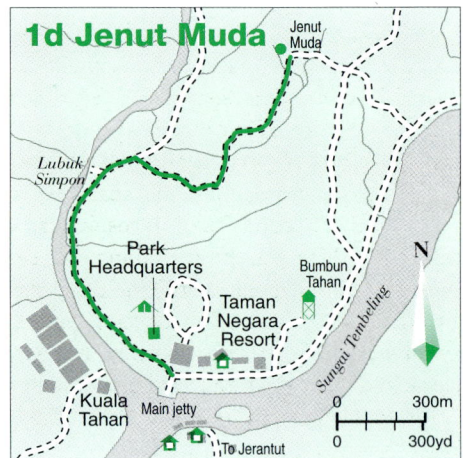

the many types of animals that visit this area. Like many animals, the Tapir is well camouflaged although it is black and white. It feeds mainly in the evening, which makes it even harder to see. Wild pigs are more commonly seen as they forage for tubers and roots. Being omnivorous they also eat reptiles, invertebrates and small mammals. Visitors to TNR can hear wild pigs at night in the forest or even under their lodges. They rarely go far from water, so the salt lick is a good location for viewing them.

Visitors willing to move slowly and wait patiently may sight or hear Banded Leaf-monkeys and White-handed Gibbons along this trail. It is also a rewarding area for birdwatchers.

From Lubuk Simpon to Jenut Muda the trail undulates along the ridge, crosses a deeply cut stream, and then traverses flat ground to the muddy area. It then crosses another small stream before climbing steeply to join the Bukit Teresek Trail.

The Jenut Muda Trail offers an ideal route for those coming down the main trail from Bukit Teresek and contemplating a swim before returning to Kuala Tahan. The journey from the summit through to Lubuk Simpon takes less than 40 minutes while it takes a little over an hour from the summit to reach Park HQ.

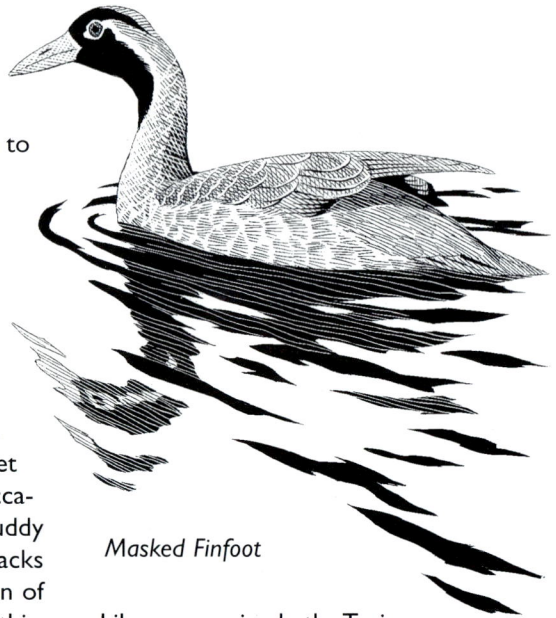

84

1e Bumbun Tabing

This return walk takes about 3 hours and forms part of the main walk to Lata Berkoh and then on to Gunung Tahan. A few sections of the trail to this hide are steep and slippery, especially after rain.

At the start of the trail, just beyond the campsite at the TNR, look for the tall green stems of ginger plants which may be flowering, producing large red pine cone-like flowers.

The trail passes the swimming hole along the Sungai Tahan called Lubuk Simpon, then the turn-off to the right to Jenut Muda and Bukit Teresek.

At dusk and dawn, Crested Fireback and Argus Pheasants may be seen along the trail, usually in family groups foraging for food on the ground. The male Argus Pheasant has a dancing ground of up to 2 square metres (21 square feet) kept bare of vegetation. Here he displays his ornamental feathers to attract a female. Seeing males and females together indicates mating pairs. Both male and female Crested Fireback have erect crests and are very dark-coloured. The male has conspicuous white tail-feathers and an overall plumage of dark bluish violet. At stream crossings look out for Chestnut-naped Forktails hopping along the water's edge. Along the riverbanks walkers should look out for Lesser Fish Eagle, Black and Red Broadbill and the skulking and secretive Masked Finfoot (the latter only from February to June). The Lesser Fish-eagle is one of 41 Malaysian birds of prey. It can often be seen perched on branches overlooking streams or rivers searching for prey in the waters below.

After the second Bukit Teresek Trail junction, the trail climbs over steep spurs before reaching the Sungai Tabing crossing. The hide is just a few minutes upstream from the crossing. Barking Deer (or Indian Muntjak) may be encountered at this lick during daylight hours. This species gets its name from the short, loud barking sound it makes, usually to frighten away predators. Other common animals to frequent the salt lick include Tapir and wild pigs, which may be seen by visitors who spend the night in the hide (see **Hides**, page 31) as they tend to be more active in their search for food after dark.

1e Bumbun Tabing

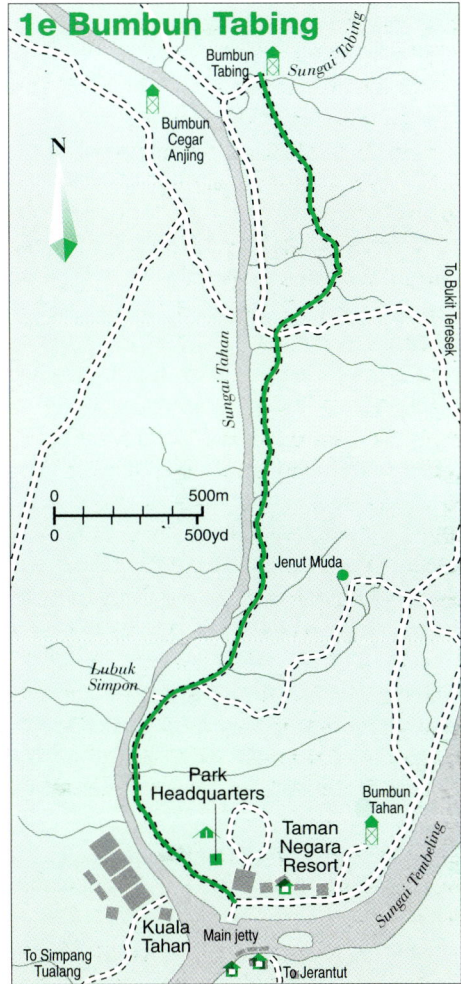

1f Rentis Neram

This trail offers a more scenic and a less steep alternative to the trail from the Bukit Teresek Junction to Bumbun Tabing Trail (note: this trail does not start from Kuala Tahan). The trail runs immediately adjacent to the east bank of Sungai Tahan, parallel to the latter part of the direct trail to Bumbun Tabing. There are many *neram* and *pelawan* trees lining Sungai Tahan here and their massive trunks, covered in epiphytes and creepers, lean far out over the water and meet with those on the opposite bank.

The trail crosses Sungai Tabing where it meets with Sungai Tahan. From this junction, Bumbun Tabing is a short walk upstream. Just downstream from the junction there is a shallow section of Sungai Tahan where it is usually not difficult to cross for those wanting to continue to Bumbun Cegar Anjing on the western banks of the river – the latter hide is 3 kilometres (2 miles) one way from Kuala Tahan.

1g Lata Berkoh

For the early sections of this trail, see the notes on the Kuala Tahan to Bumbun Tabing and Rentis Neram Trails.

The boat trip up Sungai Tahan to the cascades at Lata Berkoh is one of the most scenic and photogenic in the park. For these reasons, it is a highly recommended experience for any visitor. The trip takes about one hour and on sections of the return journey the boatman may turn the motor off for the boat to glide downstream.

On various sections of the river the fern covered trees on either side meet to form a sheltered avenue. Although the river has travelled some 50 kilometres (30 miles) from Gunung Tahan by the time it reaches the cascades, the waters are generally shallow. The rocky riverbed is suitable for paddling and wading in the cool clean waters. The waters here and in other isolated parts of the park have a slight clear tea colouring resulting from the natural decay of vegetation that falls into the river.

The cascades mark the limit for navigation along the river. Here, the bubbling waters provide an invigorating natural spa bath and the riverbanks are popular for picnics and relaxation. There is a fishing lodge and camping ground next to the river for

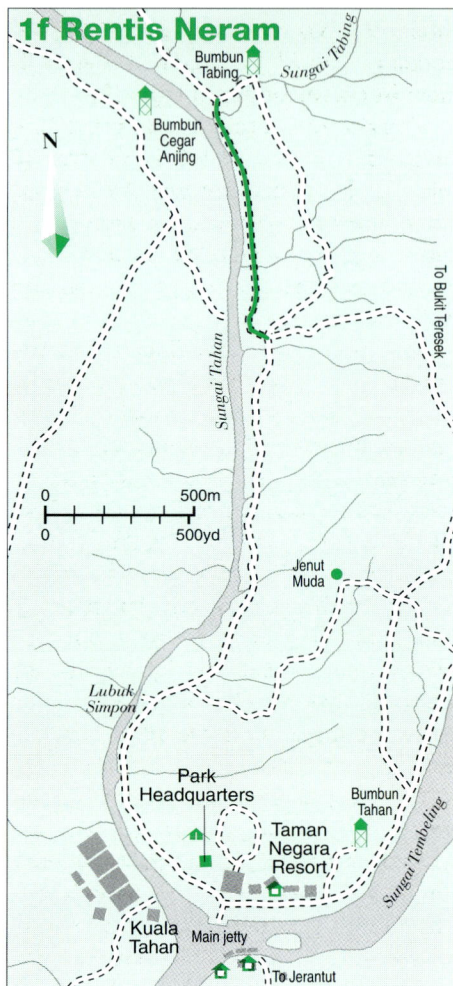
1f Rentis Neram

those who want to stay overnight, and bookings should be made at the TNR (see: **Accommodation** page 29).

The alternative to the boat trip to the cascades is a hike of 9.5 kilometres (6 miles) or 3-5 hours (one way). With stops along the route it makes a pleasant day's return walk on a well-defined trail. Many visitors take the boat up to the falls and walk back or vice versa.

The hide at Bumbun Tabing and the nearby river crossing are good places to rest and spend some time looking for animals. About ten minutes further on the trail crosses Sungai Wa and continues on to where Lubuk Lesong is reached. Turn left for a short walk to this deep swimming spot on Sungai Tahan. The broad pebbly beach and adjacent vegetation is photogenic and another good spot to relax, swim or picnic. The light conditions along the river for photography are poor so keen photograhers are advised to use fast film or a tripod

From this junction it is around 15 minutes along the main trail to the left turn to Lata Berkoh. The main trail continues on to Kuala Trenggan and Gunung Tahan. The journey to Lata Berkoh from here on follows a narrower trail that crosses several gullies and ridges. The trail leads to the banks of Sungai Tahan where boats drop off passengers. Caution needs to be exercised if the river is high and flowing rapidly. If this is the case walkers will need to be ferried across by the boatmen sitting on the opposite bank. The last 500 metres (550 yards) walk to the cascades follows the river and passes the camping grounds and the lodge.

Adventurous walkers may want to explore the pools and rapids further upstream where there is a rudimentary trail to follow.

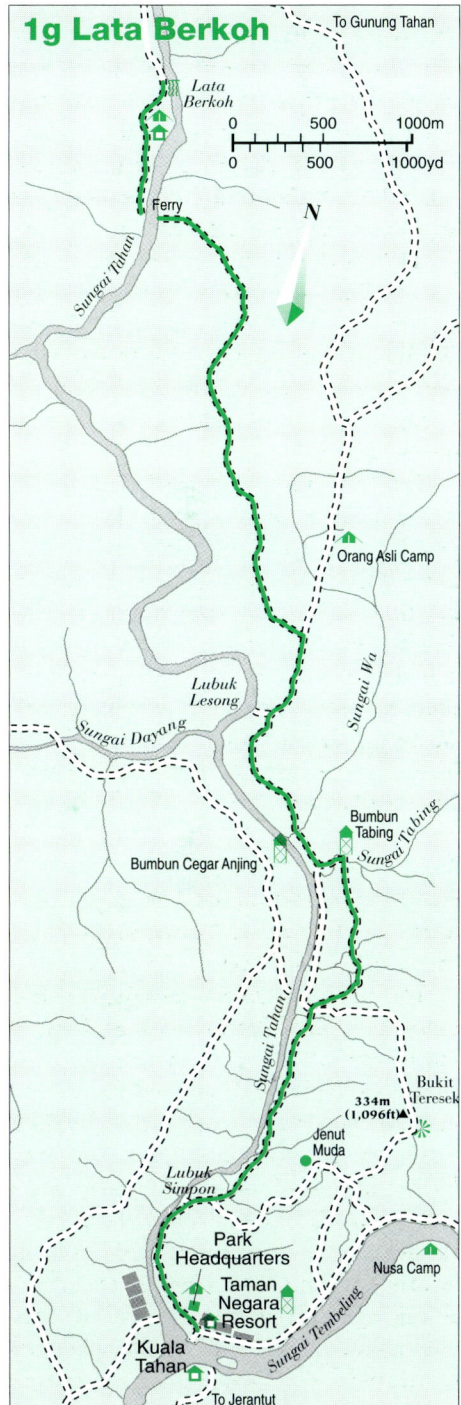

1g Lata Berkoh

2 Trails through Simpang Tualang

Simpang Tualang (Tualang Junction) is a major fork in the trail system on the western side of Sungai Tahan. From here a number of walks head north and south on the western side of Sungai Tahan and Sungai Tembeling.

The first obstacle in any of these journeys is the river crossing at the mouth of Sungai Tahan. There is a track from the TNR down the bank of Sungai Tembeling that leads to the boat re-fuelling raft right at the mouth of the Tahan. Passing boats take walkers across Sungai Tahan for a small, negotiable fee.

2a Simpang Tualang

Once across Sungai Tahan, the path on the other side leads up through the small village housing the TNR staff and their families. This path is quite steep, and walkers should allow an hour to reach the junction from park HQ. The trail into the forest begins to the left of the mosque, on the hill-slope at the back of the village. At a fork soon after Simpang Tualang the trail to the right (north) is known as Ulu Tekah, and leads to Bumbun Cegar Anjing (trail 2b) and Bumbun Tabing (the latter by crossing Sungai Tahan). The left fork leads to Gua Telinga (trail 2c) and beyond the caves to hides, hilltop views and the Rentis Tenor. The next section is a long difficult climb to the Gunung Sumpur ridge.

The walk passes large strangler figs and a giant *tualang* tree with an extensive buttressed root system and towering white trunk. At Simpang Tualang look for epiphytic ferns and large Feather-leafed Orchids high up on the branches.

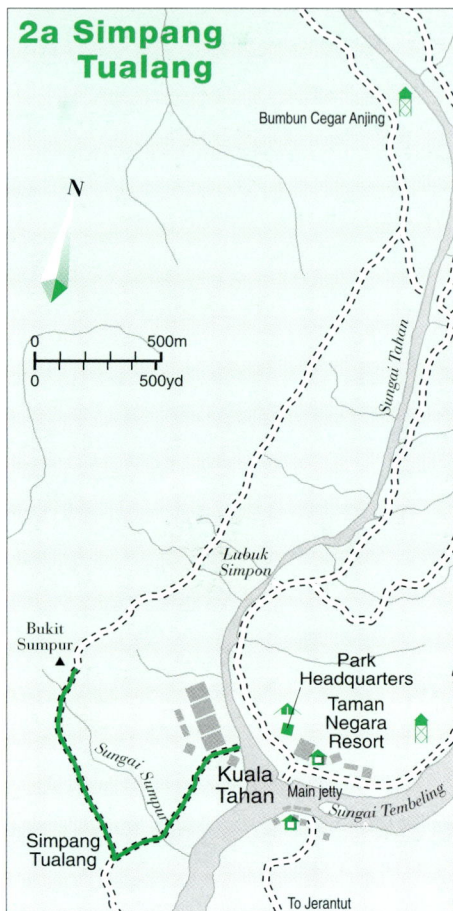

2a Simpang Tualang

Bumbun Cegar Anjing

N

0 — 500m
0 — 500yd

Sungai Tahan

Lubuk Simpon

Bukit Sumpur

Sungai Sumpur

Park Headquarters
Taman Negara Resort

Kuala Tahan   Main jetty

Simpang Tualang

Sungai Tembeling

To Jerantut

2b Simpang Tualang to Bumbun Cegar Anjing via Ulu Tekah

The three hour (one way) journey along this trail exhibits all the classic features of the tropical rainforest ecosystem. The trail is 4.5 kilometres (3 miles) in one direction and can be an alternative approach to Bumbun Tabing and a return walk to Kuala Tahan via Lubuk Simpon.

The trail crosses many small tributaries of Sungai Tekah, and eventually passes into

ABOVE: AFTER SIX DAYS TREK, FINE VIEWS REWARD THOSE WHO REACH THE SUMMIT OF GUNUNG TAHAN.

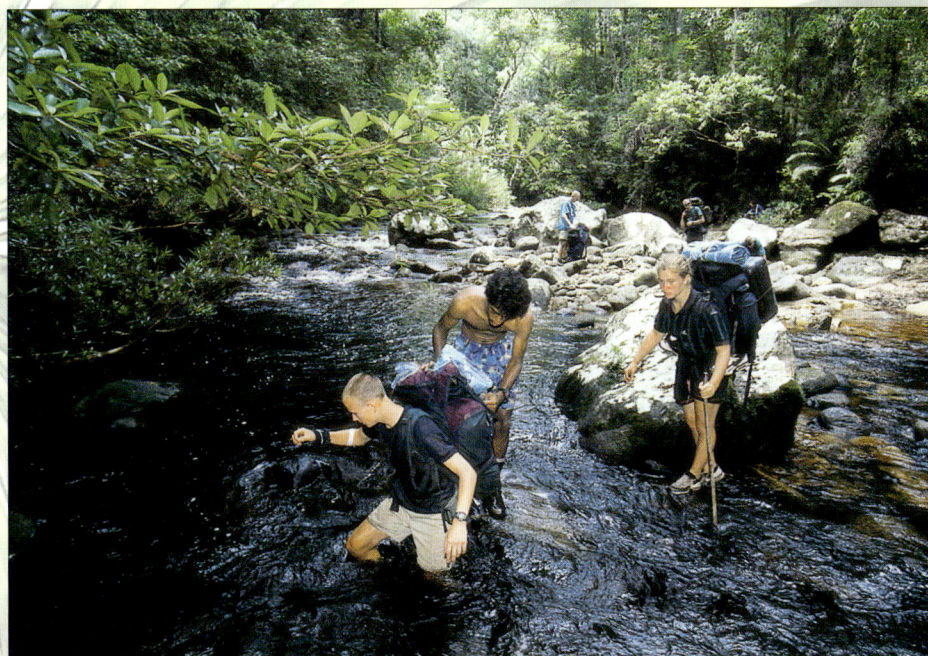
ABOVE: WALKERS ON THE LONGER TRAILS SHOULD COME PREPARED TO TACKLE A VARIETY OF TERRAIN.

LEFT: THE SOUTHERN PIED HORNBILL IS ONE OF NINE HORNBILL SPECIES RECORDED FROM THE PARK. LIKE THE OTHERS IT IS OFTEN FOUND IN THE VICINITY OF FRUITING RIVERSIDE TREES.

BELOW: THE LONG-TAILED MACAQUE IS THE MONKEY SPECIES MOST OFTEN SEEN BY VISITORS. IT USUALLY OCCURS IN TROOPS OF TEN OR MORE.

OPPOSITE ABOVE: DIPTEROCARP TREES, NAMED AFTER THEIR TWO-WINGED SEEDS, DOMINATE THE LOWLAND FORESTS OF THE PARK.

OPPOSITE BELOW LEFT: THE FEMALE GOLDEN ORB WEB SPIDER BUILDS LARGE AND VERY STRONG WEBS ACROSS GAPS IN THE UNDERGROWTH.

OPPOSITE BELOW RIGHT: FUNGI THRIVE ON THE DAMP FOREST FLOOR AND PLAY A VITAL ROLE IN BREAKING DOWN ORGANIC MATTER.

ABOVE: SALT LICKS ARE A VITAL SOURCE OF NUTRIENTS AND MINERALS, AND ATTRACT A VARIETY OF FOREST CREATURES. THESE VARY FROM LARGE MAMMALS SUCH AS THE MIGHTY SELADANG (LEFT), THE WORLD'S BIGGEST CATTLE SPECIES, TO A DAZZLING MULTITUDE OF BUTTERFLIES (RIGHT).

LEFT: THE SMALL-CLAWED OTTER IS THE SMALLER OF THE TWO OTTER SPECIES IN THE PARK. IT PREFERS SMALLER TRIBUTARIES AND STREAMS, WHEREAS ITS LARGER RELATIVE, THE SMOOTH OTTER, IS MORE OFTEN ENCOUNTERED ON BROADER STRETCHES OF RIVER.

the catchment of Sungai Dayang. One sizeable tributary of the Dayang is crossed, and then the trail branches.

The trail to the left is the Rentis Tenor (trail 5) while the trail that continues to the right is the Ulu Tekah Trail, running about 400 metres (440 yards) to another saddle, and then a kilometre or so (less than a mile) to Sungai Tahan and Bumbun Cegar Anjing.

The salt lick here is artificial and was established to attract deer and Seladang. The hide accommodates eight people.

There is some secondary vegetation here suggesting some past clearing (the site was once an airfield). As a result, the birds are different, with coucals and jungle fowl often seen. Birdwatching is good along other parts of the trail too with pittas, trogons, fire-backed pheasants, forktails, and broadbills all in evidence.

To continue on to Kuala Tahan, cross Sungai Tahan and return via the Bumbun Tabing Trail (trail 1e) or the Rentis Neram Trail (trail 1f).

2b Simpang Tualang to Bumbun Cegar Anjing via the Ulu Tekah Trail

TRAILS THROUGH SIMPANG TUALANG: 2a-2d

Start:	Park HQ at Kuala Tahan.
Finish:	Park HQ at Kuala Tahan.
Distance:	1Km (½ mile) to 40 Km (25 miles).
Duration:	1 hour to several days.
Best time:	Any time.
Conditions:	Lower altitudes: rainforest and rivers. Higher altitudes: mountain ridges and gullies.
Fitness:	Moderate fitness, especially for the longer walks.
Equipment:	Good walking shoes, raincape, leech socks and insect repellent. Binoculars and camera. Light clothing for day. If staying overnight in hides; warm clothes, food and water. If camping; camping and cooking gear, food and water. Torch and batteries for exploring caves.
Regulations:	Guides are recommended for longer trails.

Trail planner

2c Gua Telinga

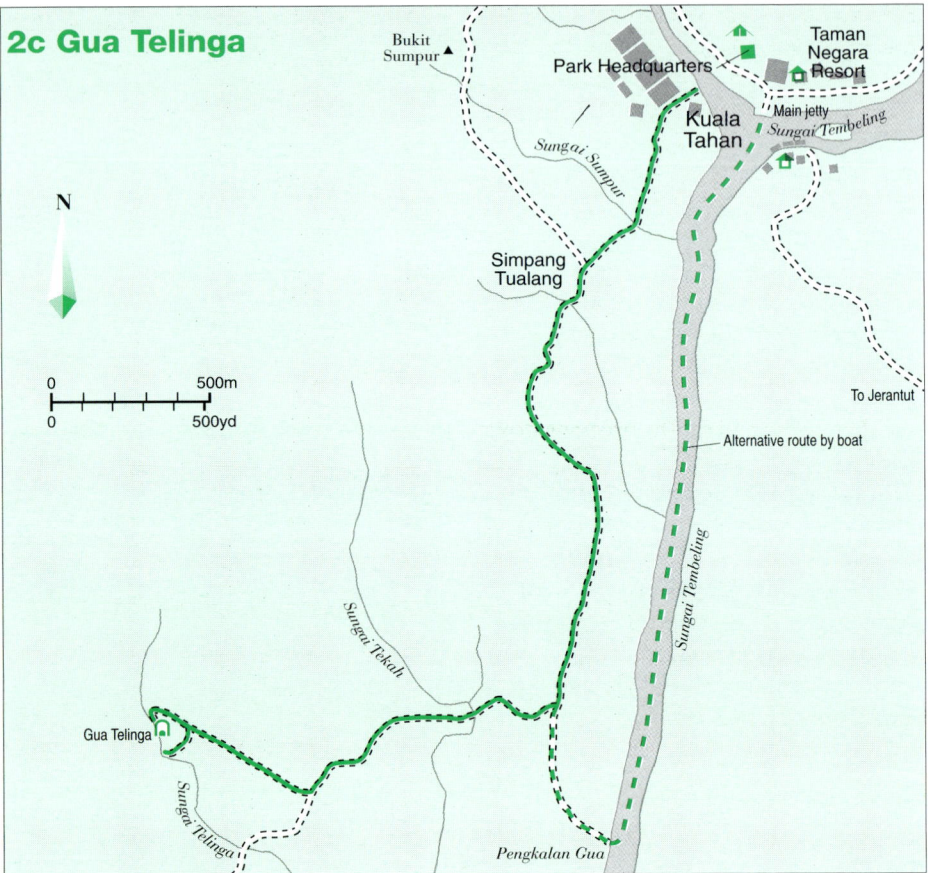

- Bukit Sumpur
- Park Headquarters
- Taman Negara Resort
- Kuala Tahan
- Main jetty
- *Sungai Tembeling*
- *Sungai Sumpur*
- Simpang Tualang
- N
- 0 — 500m
- 0 — 500yd
- To Jerantut
- Alternative route by boat
- *Sungai Tekah*
- *Sungai Tembeling*
- *Sungai Telinga*
- Gua Telinga
- *Pengkalan Gua*

2c. Gua Telinga

This limestone cave, also known as Ear Cave, is 2.6 kilometres (1½mile) walk (4 hours return) or a ten minute boat journey from the TNR to the riverbank jetty, Pengkalan Gua. From the riverbank, the caves are 30 minutes walk away along a well defined trail through the rainforest. A small sign and a wooden bench indicate the entrance. There is a rope following a stream course leading through the cave although it is recommended that visitors join a guided crawl. While the length of the cave is only about 80 metres (90 yards), there are a few narrow and difficult stretches, but most people should be able to pass through without too much difficulty. The cave may not be negotiable during heavy rains and the monsoon season.

Those who walk all the way from Kuala Tahan must first cross Sungai Tahan and walk to Simpang Tualang before taking the left-hand trail that descends to the flat river terrace along the Sungai Tembeling. The forest here looks different from that on the slopes – probably due to regular flooding. Crossing the smaller water courses, walkers should look out for the White-crowned Forktails that are found here.

The cave is home to bats, frogs, insects and Cave Racer Snakes (*Elaphe taeniura*).

Bats are the most significant animals in the cave system and usually the only ones that leave the cave for food. There are two species; the Roundleaf (*Hipposideros larvatus*) and Dusky Fruit Bat (*Penthetor lucasi*). Accumulations of bat guano on the cave floor are the food source for a very delicately balanced food chain. Bats serve a very important role in pollinating fruit trees and supplying nutrients to the cave ecosystem.

In a cave rich in bats, the floor crawls with flies, maggots, millipedes, worms, roaches, mites and moths breaking down the bat guano. These organisms are in turn eaten by those further up the food chain, such as small mammals, frogs (e.g. the Black-striped – *Rana nigrovittata*) and toads (e.g. the Giant Toad – *Bufo asper*). At the top of this chain is the Cave Racer, the only snake adapted to spending its whole life in a cave. It feeds almost exclusively on bats and swiftlets.

2d Gua Telinga to Bumbun Belau and Bumbun Yong

Visitors to Gua Telinga can walk via Simpang Tualang or arrive by boat at Pengkalan Gua on Sungai Tembeling. This walk can be done in reverse from Bumbun Belau (or Blau) and Yong by taking a boat to Pengkalan Belau and walking back towards Gua Telinga.

From Pengkalan Gua and the river, the trail crosses a wooden bridge and ten minutes further on branches, with tracks to the right (towards Simpang Tualang) and to the left (to Bumbun Belau and Yong). Gua Telinga lies straight ahead.

To reach Bumbun Belau and Yong, proceed left and cross the stream that flows from Gua Telinga. The trail crosses undulating country through tall forests before reaching Bumbun Belau.

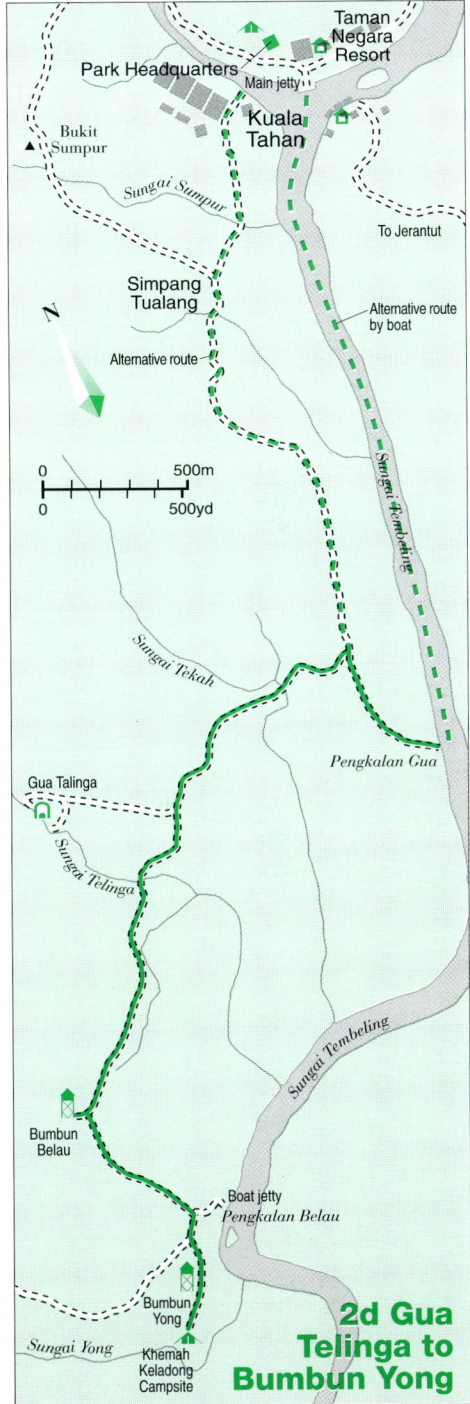

Taman Negara Resort
Park Headquarters
Main jetty
Kuala Tahan
Bukit Sumpur
Sungai Sumpur
To Jerantut
Simpang Tualang
Alternative route by boat
N
Alternative route
0   500m
0   500yd
Sungai Tembeling
Sungai Tekah
Pengkalan Gua
Gua Talinga
Sungai Telinga
Bumbun Belau
Sungai Tembeling
Boat jetty
Pengkalan Belau
Bumbun Yong
Sungai Yong
Khemah Keladong Campsite

2d Gua Telinga to Bumbun Yong

Ten minutes on from Bumbun Belau trekkers reach a T-junction. To the left, steps lead down to the boat jetty of Pengkalan Belau on Sungai Tembeling. To the right the main trail leads to Bumbun Yong (ten minutes).

Tapir are often seen here, before dawn. Barking and Sambar Deer are also common visitors, and any rustling below the hide is most likely to be Civet Cats. Bumbun Belau has six bunks and a toilet but you should bring your own water from Kuala Tahan. Bumbun Yong has eight bunks, toilet and water collected from the roof.

2e Khemah (Camp) Keladong and Bukit Pecah Piring

Both destinations are accessible from Kuala Tahan via Simpang Tualang, Gua Telinga, Bumbun Belau and Bumbun Yong (trails 2a–2d). From Bumbun Yong the steep 2 kilometre (1¼ mile) trail takes about 75 minutes one way.

Beyond Bumbun Yong, a narrow trail winds on for a few hundred metres to a fork. To the left at the fork the trail continues for roughly 500 metres (540 yards) to Khemah Keladong, a good campsite on a terraced bank adjoining Sungai Yong.

To the right is a trail leading to a point on the Yong River upstream from Khemah Keladong. There is a good campsite here that is accessible by walking along the banks or wading through the shallow stream. The stream is crossed, and the trail to the conical-shaped Bukit Pecah Piring (Broken-saucer Hill) continues through undulating terrain and lowland forest and then starts climbing to the 308 metre (1,010 feet) summit of the mountain. The climb is only 250 metres (800 feet) high as the base is already some distance above sea level. There are no views to be had from this summit.

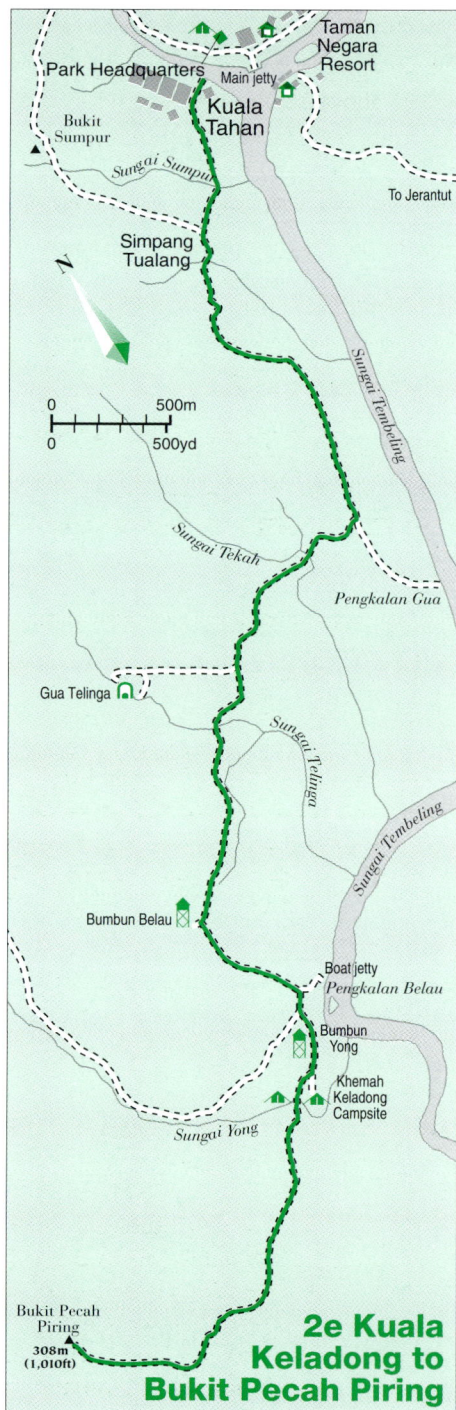

Taman Negara Resort

Park Headquarters Main jetty

Kuala Tahan

Bukit Sumpur

Sungai Sumpur

To Jerantut

Simpang Tualang

N

Sungai Tembeling

0   500m
0   500yd

Sungai Tekah

Pengkalan Gua

Gua Telinga

Sungai Telinga

Sungai Tembeling

Bumbun Belau

Boat jetty
Pengkalan Belau

Bumbun Yong

Khemah Keladong Campsite

Sungai Yong

Bukit Pecah Piring
308m
(1,010ft)

2e Kuala Keladong to Bukit Pecah Piring

3 Trails to Kuala Trenggan

Two trails link Park HQ with Kuala Trenggan to the north. Either makes an excellent one day walk, returning by river. Alternatively the two form a good two day round trip, staying at the lodge at Kuala Trenggan or at Bumbun Kumbang overnight.

3a Kuala Trenggan via Gunung Indah

Keen walkers can walk 9 kilometres (5 ½ miles) to the lodge and then take a thrilling sampan ride back through the Tembeling Gorge and seven rapids (Nusa, Dua, Abai, Teras, Dedari, Panjang and Trenggan) along Sungai Tembeling or vice versa. The boat journey takes about 45 minutes and covers about 10 kilometres (6 miles). Otters may be seen in these rapids swimming rapidly and catching fish. Hornbills and fish eagles often pass overhead.

Most visitors take the boat to Kuala Trenggan and back through the rapids. Be prepared to get a little wet, so protect any valuables such as cameras. Lodge accommodation is available at Kuala Trenggan but bookings should be made at the TNR before setting off. The lodge is a lot smaller and quieter than the TNR and there are limited facilities. It sits high above the river and is an ideal location for those who want to escape crowds.

This first part of the trail to Kuala Trenggan follows the course of the Sungai Tembeling and the Canopy Walk Trail (trail 1a). From here, it involves many steep ascents and descents and is only recommended for those who are physically fit and with good walking shoes. The trip usually takes four to six hours from Kuala Tahan. It can take longer if side-trips are taken to the look-outs on Gunung Indah (Beautiful Hill) with its interesting vegetation and spectacular views, or to one of several waterfalls along the way. The return trip to Gunung Indah from Kuala Tahan can be done in about four hours, but like all trails in the park, there is a lot to see along the way so plan a little extra time.

TRAILS TO KUALA TRENGGAN: 3a – 3b

Start:	Park HQ at Kuala Tahan.
Finish:	Kuala Trenggan.
Distance:	9Km (5½ miles) or 12Km (7½ miles).
Duration:	One day
Best time:	February or March
Conditions:	Lower altitudes: rainforest and rivers. Higher altitudes: mountain ridges and gullies
Fitness:	Best for moderate to experienced trekkers
Equipment:	Light clothing, trekking boots and raincape. Leech socks and insect repellent. Binoculars and camera.
Regulations:	Guides are recommended.

Trail planner

TAMAN NEGARA

The trail beyond the Canopy Walk skirts rock walls and boulders in very steep country, and then climbs sharply up to a T-intersection along a narrow ridge. The righthand path leads down to the Sungai Tembeling and a deep pool called Lubuk Udang (Prawn Pool). From here a branch trail goes on to Kuala Trenggan.

Back on the ridge, the left hand path is a steep trail leading up the Gunung Indah ridge to the base of a narrow out-crop of glass-like, quartzite rock. Quartzite is a metamorphic rock that is extremely hard and weathers more slowly than the surrounding rock and, as a result, stands out. Walkers should exer-cise caution on the steep climb to the look-out.

At the look-out the environment changes dramatically from lowland rain-forest to exposed cliffs with stunted vegetation growing on thin soils. Scientists still have much to learn about this unique environment. The soils are poor and infertile due to the slow ero-sion rates of the parent rock. Another problem for plant survival here is that of drought. This may sound odd in the mid-dle of a rainforest, but a few days with-out rain in a rainforest can severely affect plants sensitive to moisture reten-tion.

The vegetation on Gunung Indah is unique so all visitors here need to be very careful about conserving the species that inhabit the area. One interesting plant is the red, papery-barked tree that belongs to the *Eugenia* genus.

The upper and lower look-outs overlook Lubuk Udang and the roaring rapids, Jeram Nusa, about 120 metres (400 feet) below. The trail to the summit of Gunung Indah is a dead-end and walkers have to retrace their steps to the base of the moun-tain.

There are several options for visiting Gunung Indah. Visitors can walk part of the way and travel by boat for the rest. For example, boats travelling up the Sungai

3a Kuala Trenggan via Gunung Indah

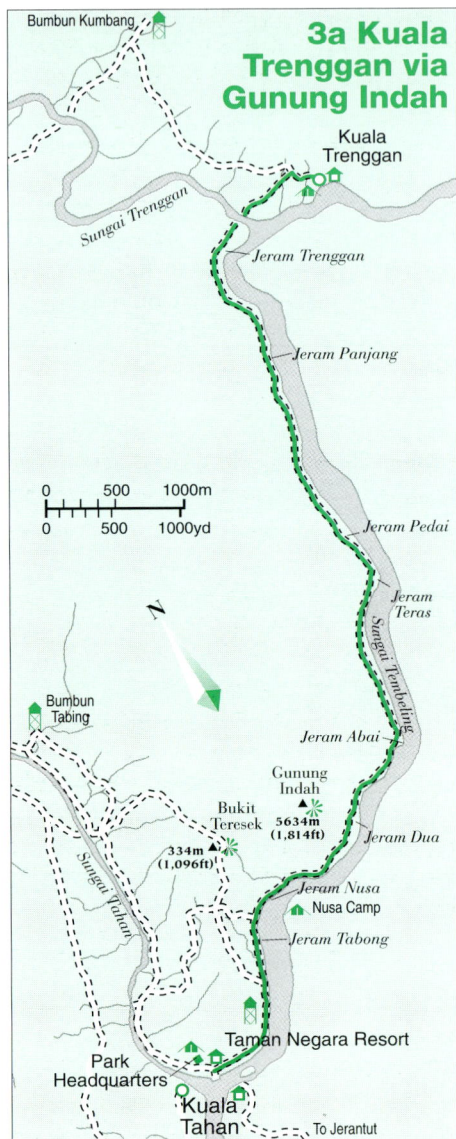

98

Tembeling can drop off or pick up passengers at Lubuk Udang. This means visitors can walk to the mountain and then catch a boat out or vice versa.

Beyond Gunung Indah the trail enters more rugged country, and some sections may be difficult after rain. While the trail is well above the river in many places, there are lower sections from which it is possible to side-track down to the water's edge.

At the second permanent stream crossed after the Gunung Indah ridge there is a large rock overhang beside a narrow, deep pool. From the trail and up the stream bed there is a small waterfall some 15 minutes wade upstream.

One kilometre (½ mile) further along the trail reaches Sungai Trenggan. This is crossed by means of a raft on a fixed rope. It is safest for only one person to cross at a time. Just 150 metres (170 yards) more along the trail and there is a junction with Kuala Trenggan five minutes walk to the right and Bumbun Kumbang about 40 minutes walk to the left.

Kuala Trenggan is in a beautiful location high above Sungai Tembeling. There are 10 wooden chalets, each sleeping a few people. There is also a simple restaurant and the facilities are quite comfortable for those looking for a peaceful rainforest retreat. An adjoining campsite offers a cheaper alternative for backpackers.

3b Kuala Trenggan via Bumbun Kumbang and Rentis Tahan

This is the inland western route to Kuala Trenggan and it is advisable to allow six hours leisurely walk to the hide at Bumbun Kumbang and a little under seven hours to Kuala Trenggan. An alternative route for those who just want to reach the hide at Kumbang is to catch a boat to Kuala Trenggan and walk the remaining 45 minutes.

From Kuala Tahan the trail runs parallel with Sungai Tahan, past Bumbun Tabing to the turn-off to Lubuk Lesong. This is about one third of the journey to Bumbun Kumbang. Trail notes on the sections between Kuala Tahan and Lata Berkoh are described under walks 1e and 1g.

Between Lubok Lesong and Sungai Trenggan excellent stands of lowland dipterocarp forest are traversed. The trail is fairly straight, with several small stream crossings and two side trails to the left to Lata Berkoh and Gunung Tahan.

The trail beyond the Gunung Tahan junction climbs a gentle rise over the divide between Sungai Tahan and Sungai Trenggan. Then there is a descent and several more small stream crossings until the trail reaches Sungai Trenggan. Normally Sungai Trenggan is

Water Monitor Lizard

no more than knee-deep but it could be impassable after rainstorms especially in months when the rainfall is higher. The river makes a pleasant spot for hot and tired walkers to stop and rest. There are excellent swimming holes to take a relaxing swim or just to soak aching feet.

Elephant tracks can be spotted along the way. Their size should give them away and the large, soccer-ball size droppings shouldn't be too hard for most people to identify.

The walk to Bumbun Kumbang is about another 20 minutes from the crossing and from there, a little under an hour's gentle walk to the lodge at Kuala Trenggan. The hide at Kumbang is more open than the others in the park and Seladang (wild cattle) have been seen here. Seladang were once hunted by colonialists at the beginning of the century but they are now a

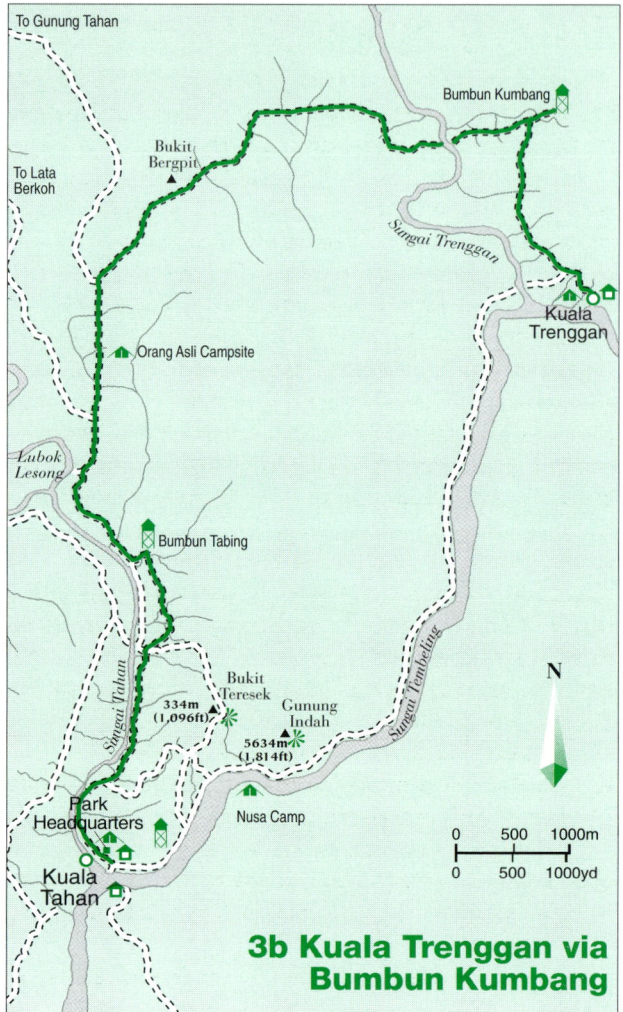

3b Kuala Trenggan via Bumbun Kumbang

protected species. Taman Negara offers a large and safe habitat, with only tigers being a threat to their young. During the day Seladang seek the cool of the forest venturing out into the open grassed areas and to the salt licks at dusk. Herds of half a dozen or so animals may be seen but more often than not the only sign will be hoof marks in the soft muddy areas. More common are Tapir, Sambar and Barking Deer. The hide has six bunks, a toilet and rainwater is collected from the roof.

Another option for this adventure is a full day loop, travelling up by boat and walking back, or vice versa. If time is not an obstacle, spend two days trekking via Rentis Tahan to either an overnight stay in the lodge at Kuala Trenggan or in the hide at Kumbang, and on day two return to Kuala Tahan via Gunung Indah and the Tembeling Gorge (this is walk 3a in reverse).

4 Trails around Kuala Keniam

North of Kuala Trenggan, trails continue to Kuala Keniam, and from there on to Kuala Perkai. Once again, the return journeys can be made by boat.

4a Kuala Trenggan/Bumbun Kumbang to Kuala Keniam

Kuala Trenggan can be reached either by walking or by boat. The easiest on the muscles is to catch a boat from Kuala Tahan to the lodge. Of the two walking tracks, one comes up the Tembeling Gorge via the Canopy Walk and Gunung Indah. The inland route goes up Sungai Tahan and down Sungai Trenggan via Bumbun Kumbang (walk 3b).

The walk to Kuala Keniam is about 20 kilometres (12 miles) from Kuala Trenggan and 18 kilometres (11 miles) from Bumbun Kumbang. The walk can be done in one day providing there is little exploring along the way. However, a more relaxed alternative is to spend two days to look at things and camp out on the trail beside a stream. The trail can conveniently be divided into three sections: Bumbun Kumbang to Kepayang; Kepayang to Batu Luas; Batu Luas to Kuala Keniam. A total walking time of two to three hours should be allowed for each section.

The first section runs parallel with the Trenggan Valley, affording occasional glimpses of the river. The terrain is undulating, with some steep hillsides, and the dipterocarp forest houses occasional clumps of dense bamboo. The low-lying trail then crosses several limestone outcrops, and finally passes through rolling hills to Kuala Keniam.

Near the southern end of the limestone hill, Batu Kepayang, the trail turns to the right, and a side trail continues straight ahead, crossing a stream and ending at the entrance to Gua Kepayang Kecil (Small Kepayang Cave). There are some good places to camp along this stretch. It is about two and a half hours walk from Kuala Trenggan.

The cave interiors are attractive, although graffiti has somewhat spoilt their natural beauty. Gua Kepayang Besar (Big Kepayang Cave) is the main cave here and is reached by a left hand turn a little further along the trail. This is quite a large chamber, with

KUALA TRENGGAN/BUMBUN KUMBANG TO KUALA KENIAM AND KUALA PERKIA: 4a – 4b

Start: Kuala Trenggan.
Finish: Kuala Keniam or Kuala Perkai.
Distance: 20Km (12 miles) to 24.5Km (15 miles).
Duration: One to two days.
Best time: February or March.
Conditions: Undulating terrain. Limestone caves.
Fitness: Moderate fitness.
Equipment: Light clothing for day; Trekking boots and raincape. Torch and batteries. Adequate food and water. Leech socks and insect repellent. Binoculars and camera.
Regulations: Permits for fishing.

Trail planner

room inside to move around.

From here the next section of the walk is dominated by limestone vegetation. Although the environment looks harsh and inhospitable, limestone outcrops are very rich in plant species. In the nooks and crannies of the jagged ridges specific plants have adapted to a unique microclimate. The trail follows the southern edge of these craggy limestone hills. The milky coloured limestone bedrock is visible in the beds of streams crossed along the trail.

The next section of the trail is relatively flat, and passes two more limestone outcrops, Batu Subuh and Batu Gua Sungai. Batu Subuh rises some 100 metres (330 feet) above the forest floor. Batu Gua Sungai is notable for the stream that cuts right through the outcrop for a distance of about 50 metres (50 yards). Adventurous cavers can crawl through the cave and get a closer look at the Horseshoe

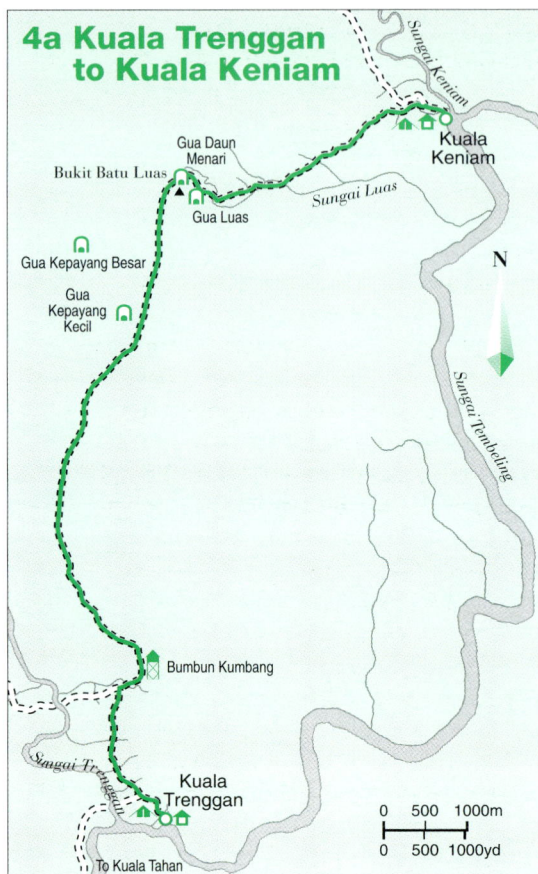

4a Kuala Trenggan to Kuala Keniam

Bats *(Rhinolophus affinis)* clinging to the cave ceiling.

At the far north-east end of Batu Gua Sungai the trail crosses the dividing ridge between the Trenggan and Keniam Valleys, although this may not be readily apparent. The next outcrop, Batu Luas, is another kilometre (half a mile) along the trail. At its north-east corner the trail links with the path from Kuala Keniam. Here, at the base of a limestone cliff, there is a good camp area beside Sungai Luas.

The large cave Daun Menari is situated near the cliff base a little distance away and there is a 30 minute walk along the base of the outcrop. Charcoal drawings on the walls have been attributed to the Orang Asli and are comparatively recent.

For rock climbers there are at least two climbs to the top of Batu Luas. One starts a few hundred metres south of the campsite and the other from just beyond the entrance to Gua Daun Menari. While no special equipment is required, the ascent should only be attempted by reasonably experienced climbers. Climbers should drink lots of water before, during and after climbing as it is quite debilitating.

The last section of the trail to Kuala Keniam leaves the flat limestone country and traverses rolling hills and lowland rainforest where tall *meranti* trees are common. The trail also crosses several rivers with freshwater suitable for bathing and drinking. The Keniam Lodge, at the junction of Sungai Keniam and Sungai Tembeling, is a very welcome sight after such a long walk. Here there are ten wooden chalets with facilities and an adjoining campsite.

4b Kuala Keniam to Kuala Perkai

This 4.5 kilometre (3 mile) trail leaves the lodge and Sungai Tembeling behind and follows Sungai Keniam through some very beautiful terrain. The walk is relatively easy although a little undulating and should only take two and a half hours, one way. There are several places where walkers can leave the trail and get down to Sungai Keniam.

Some magnificent big trees grow along the way; *merbau*, *tualang* and *neram*, in particular. In these trees and others within the forest, observant walkers may see or hear White-handed Gibbons, Banded and Dusky Leaf-monkeys as well as Long-tailed Macaques in the canopy high above their heads as they go about their daily social interactions and search for food. Monkeys and gibbons are the great "showmen" of the rainforests as their antics can entertain visitors to the park for hours. Most species of primate are social animals that live in family groups or troops, although groups of gibbons are generally smaller

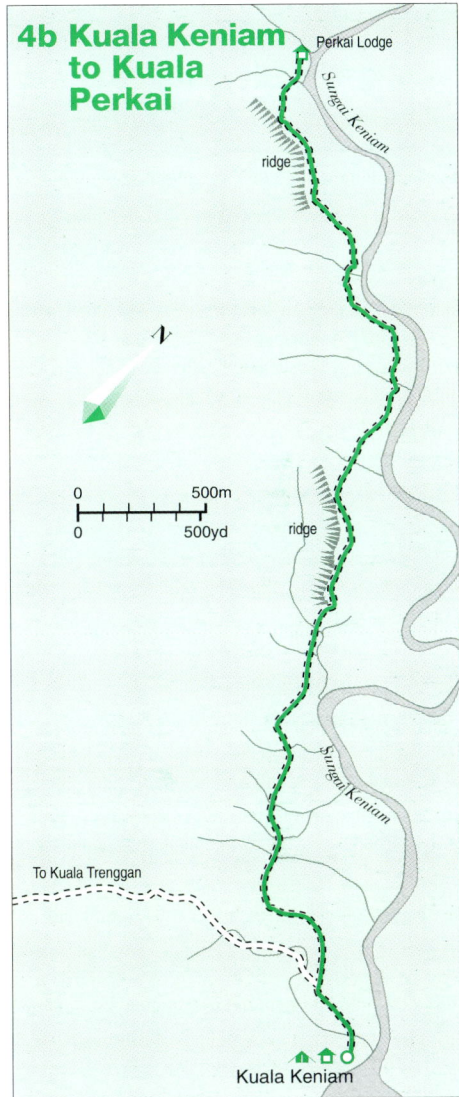

The trail ends at Perkai Lodge which is pleasantly situated overlooking the junction of Sungai Keniam and Sungai Perkai. This is the most isolated outpost on the Pahang side of the park and bookings should be made prior to leaving the TNR. The lodge is equipped with crockery, cooking utensils, firewood and water.

The alternative route to Kuala Perkai is by boat on Sungai Keniam. This is a quieter river trip than on Sungai Tahan to Lata Berkoh, and takes about two hours, depending upon the water level. The river is a series of rapids and pools and in the dry season everyone has to help push the boat through the shallow reaches – so wear some old sneakers for the occasion.

5 Rentis Tenor (Tenor Trail)

It is recommended that a guide be taken on this walk as the 35 kilometre (22 mile) long trail is unclear in places and passes through remote parts of the park. For this journey walkers need to be physically fit, and well equipped for hiking and camping.

For those who have three days to spare, this is a good trail as it is possible to visit Gua Telinga, call in at two hides (Bumbun Belau and Bumbun Yong), climb a 569 metre (1,867 feet) hill covered with montane forest, pass rapids and deep pools along Sungai Tenor, and pass through some magnificent rainforest. There are several campsites along the way in picturesque settings.

Rentis Tenor proper starts from a point about 150 metres (160 yards) from Pengkalan Belau, along the trail to Bumbun Yong. To reach this point on foot from Kuala Tahan can take half a day, or alternatively, ten minutes by boat.

Initially Rentis Tenor runs up the valley of Sungai Yong. After about two hours of traversing flat country it crosses to the west bank of Sungai Yong. After another 30 minutes it reaches the point where a side trail leads off to the left to Bukit Guling Gendang (Rolling-Drum Hill). Five minutes straight on from here a small stream is crossed, and immediately you come to a campsite, Khemah Yong.

For those who walk from Kuala Tahan it is possible to reach Khemah Yong in a day even allowing for side trips to Gua Telinga and Bumbun Yong.

Bukit Guling Gendang is a steep, arduous ascent that is best climbed early the next morning in the cool of the day. It is about an hour's climb, with the final section across fairly rocky terrain.

Towards the summit the vegetation is stunted as it grows on a peat soil. Plants of the mountain forest appear, such as the conifer *Dacrydium beccarii* and a carnivorous pitcher plant *(Nepenthes sanguinea)* climbing in the undergrowth. Both occur here at an altitude more than 400 metres (1,300 feet) lower than they do on Gunung Tahan.

From the trig point at the summit, to the north and northwest it may be possible

RENTIS TENOR

Start:	Park HQ at Kuala Tahan.
Finish:	Park HQ at Kuala Tahan.
Distance:	35Km. (22 miles), return.
Duration:	Three days.
Best time:	February or March
Conditions:	Lower altitudes: rainforest and rivers. Mountain ridges and gullies.
Fitness:	Best for experienced trekkers
Equipment:	Light clothing for day. Trekking boots and raincape. Camping and cooking gear, food and water. Torch and batteries. Leech socks and insect repellent. Binoculars and camera.
Regulations:	Guides are recommended.

Trail planner

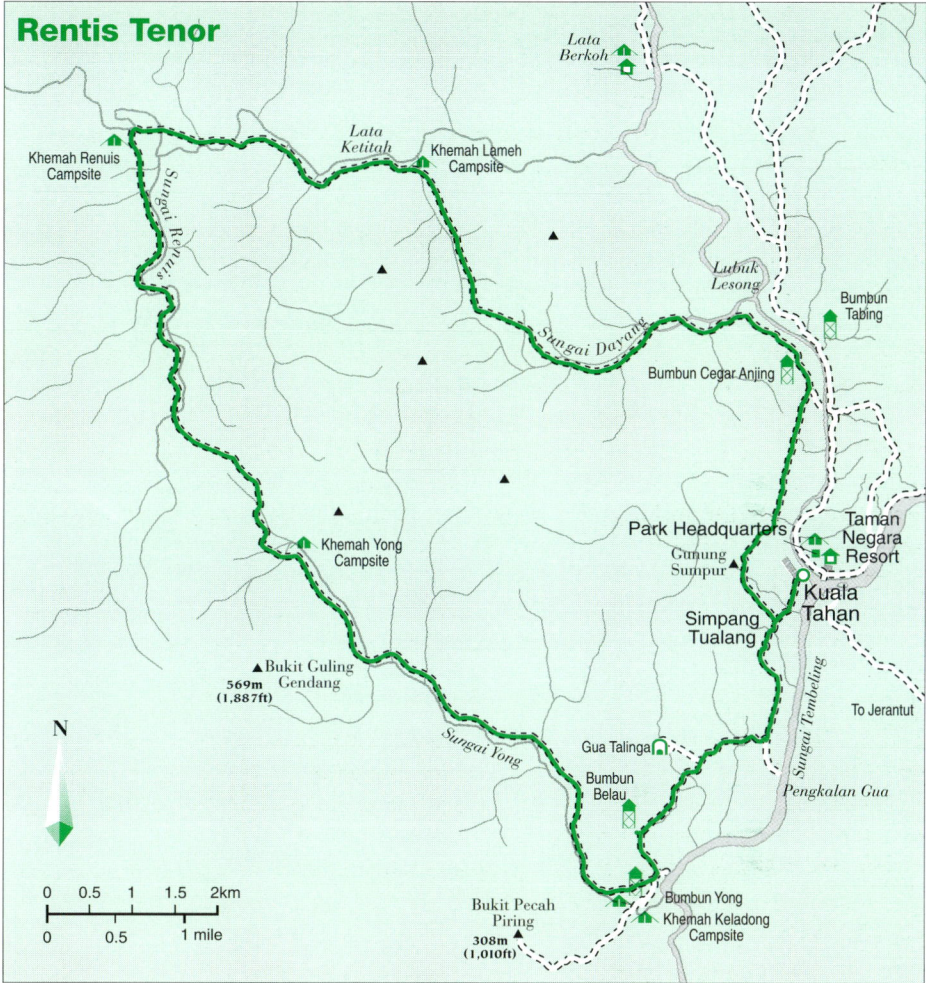

Rentis Tenor

Map labels:
- Lata Berkoh
- Khemah Renuis Campsite
- Lata Ketitah
- Khemah Lameh Campsite
- Sungai Renuis
- Sungai Dayang
- Lubuk Lesong
- Bumbun Tabing
- Bumbun Cegar Anjing
- Khemah Yong Campsite
- Park Headquarters
- Gunung Sumpur
- Taman Negara Resort
- Kuala Tahan
- Simpang Tualang
- Bukit Guling Gendang 569m (1,887ft)
- Sungai Yong
- Gua Talinga
- Bumbun Belau
- Sungai Tembeling
- To Jerantut
- Pengkalan Gua
- N
- Bukit Pecah Piring 308m (1,010ft)
- Bumbun Yong
- Khemah Keladong Campsite
- 0   0.5   1   1.5   2km
- 0   0.5   1 mile

to see Gunung Tahan and the adjoining peaks above Gua Siput and Gua Tumpat. In the distance, the highest limestone outcrop in Peninsular Malaysia, Gua Peningat – 713 metres (2,340 feet) – can be seen.

The return journey is the same as the ascent trail so there is no need to carry full packs to the top. Drinks, a snack and a camera are all that are necessary.

From Khemah Yong, Rentis Tenor continues into the upper catchment of Sungai Yong, then over a low saddle into the catchment of Sungai Renuis. From here the path runs along the Renuis, crossing it several times, until Sungai Tenor is reached. This section of the trip takes about 3 hours.

The route along Sungai Tenor may follow several trails so it is important to have the assistance of an experienced guide to avoid any possibility of getting lost. The trail follows the southern side of the river, crossing a tributary stream before reaching the next campsite, Khemah Renuis.

Pitcher plants are very interesting plants found in several locations in Asia, islands in the Indian Ocean and northern Australia. In Malaysia, there are some 30 species (3 endemic to Peninsular Malaysia and 12 endemic to East Malaysia).

Nepenthes macfarlenei is one of three species of pitcher plant known from Gunung Tahan. It is confined to the moss forest high up on the mountain, and the pale form may be distinguished from other species by the cream-coloured upper pitchers.

As pitcher plants supplement their mineral intake by trapping and digesting insects, they can survive in soils that are poor in minerals. Insects are attracted to the sugary secretions that accumulate at the base of the funnel-like plant. The outer waxy rim of the pitcher has evolved so that any insect that enters finds it difficult to escape. The sugary secretions contain enzymes that break down the bodies of trapped insects. A canopy above the pitcher prevents too much rainfall entering the plant and 'drowning' it.

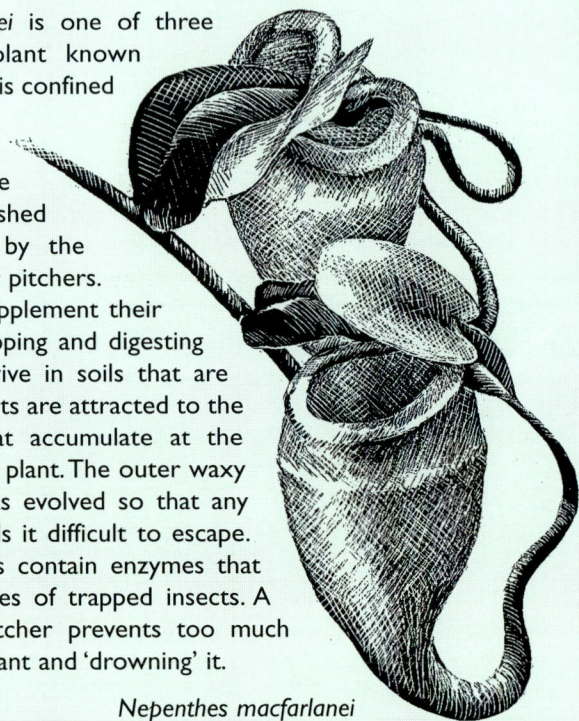

Nepenthes macfarlanei

Further downstream from this campsite Sungai Tenor flows through steep countryside and a long cascade called Lata Ketitah can be seen. The trail skirts around the hillside above the rapids, eventually descending where another tributary stream, Sungai Lameh, enters Sungai Tenor. There is another campsite here: Khemah Lameh.

At this point the trail leaves Sungai Tenor and follows Sungai Lameh and the valley of the Sungai Dayang. The latter is a tributary of Sungai Tahan. From this point the journey is downhill, following Sungai Dayang through lowland rainforest until the trail leaves the stream and cuts across flat land to join Rentis Ulu Tekah. There are several places to relax on the banks or swim in the rivers along the trail. All are well upstream of any human settlements or activity and the water is refreshingly clear except after heavy downfalls.

It is about the same distance and takes about the same time to return to Kuala Tahan via the eastern side of Sungai Tahan, crossing below Bumbun Cegar Anjing, or via Rentis Ulu Tekah.

6 Gunung Tahan from Kuala Tahan

Gunung Tahan at 2,187 metres (7,176 feet) above sea level is located in the Tahan Range and is the largest mountain in Peninsular Malaysia. There are three routes up Gunung Tahan: from Kuala Tahan, from Merapoh and from Kuala Koh. The Merapoh access is described later. Details of the Kuala Koh – Gunung Tahan – Kuala Koh Trail (constructed by Operation Raleigh) are best obtained from the Ranger Station at Kuala Koh. The Kuala Koh to Gunung Tahan return walk normally takes 16 days.

These are arduous treks demanding good physical fitness and mental determination, in addition to well maintained equipment, thorough preparation, and sound leadership if a large group is involved. Weight is crucial when it has to be carried for many days, so food should have minimal packaging and moisture content. To protect the forest, timber fires are not permissible and cooking gas or fuel must, therefore, be carried as well. All rubbish must be accounted for, except for materials that can be burned. It is best to eliminate all non-essential packaging before leaving Kuala Tahan.

The 110 kilometre (70 mile) return walk from Kuala Tahan to the mountain summit normally takes eight to nine days. The trail passes several river crossings, sometimes hazardous, and traverses long dry ridges demanding rationing of every last drop of water. The climatic extremes are daunting, as conditions on the Gunung Tahan plateau can be very cold, whereas in the lowlands, the high humidity is debilitating. Rains can be very heavy and prolonged.

All groups are required to employ the services of a guide as the path is not always apparent. Each guide accompanies a maximum of 12 trekkers. Porters and guides

GUNUNG TAHAN FROM KUALA TAHAN

Trail planner

Start:	Park HQ at Kuala Tahan.
Finish:	Gunung Tahan, then return to Park HQ.
Distance:	55 km (35 miles) each way.
Duration:	7-9 days round trip with extensions of up to 16 days.
Best time:	February or March
Conditions:	Lower altitudes: rainforest and rivers. Higher altitudes: mountain ridges and gullies. Cold at night on the peak.
Fitness:	Best for experienced trekkers
Equipment:	Light clothing for day; warm clothes for mountain nights (no shelter). Trekking boots and raincape. Camping and cooking gear, food and water. Torch and batteries. Leech socks and insect repellent. Binoculars and camera.
Regulations:	Guide compulsory. 12 people or more require two guides. Trek and camera permits required.

receive a weekly fee and payment of this is shared by the group. If you are travelling in a small group it may be possible to join others to share these costs. Because of limited space at some campsites and increasingly heavy use of this trail it is suggested that there should be no more than twelve people in a group.

All groups should report to reception on arrival in Taman Negara, to arrange a briefing by DWNPPN park staff.

The recommended schedule for this trip covers eight days, allowing time for walkers to replenish their energy, relax and absorb the superb natural surroundings. A faster pace is possible, but tends to result in exhaustion and diminishes appreciation of the route.

Day One — Kuala Tahan to Sungai Melantai

Day Two — Sungai Melanti to Kuala Puteh

Day Three — Kuala Puteh to Kuala Teku

Day Four — Kuala Teku to Wray's Camp (or further on to Skeat's Ridge)

Day Five — Wray's Camp/Skeat's Ridge to Padang Camp

Day Six — Padang Camp to Gunung Tahan and descent to Kuala Teku

Day Seven — Kuala Teku to Kuala Puteh

Day Eight — Kuala Putah to Kuala Tahan

Kuala Tahan to Melantai River.

Allow five hours for this section. The main inland trail from Park HQ to Kuala Trenggan (Rentis Tahan to Trenggan) is followed for about two hours through undulating lowland forest. Lubuk Lesong,

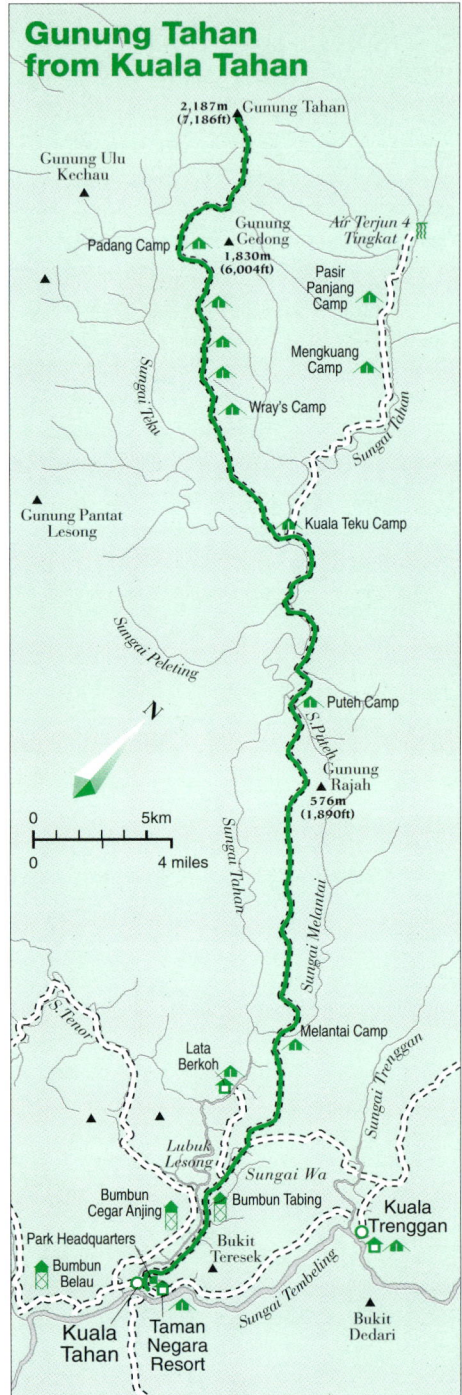

Gunung Tahan from Kuala Tahan

2,187m (7,186ft) Gunung Tahan
Gunung Ulu Kechau
Gunung Gedong 1,830m (6,004ft)
Padang Camp
Air Terjun 4 Tingkat
Pasir Panjang Camp
Mengkuang Camp
Wray's Camp
Sungai Teku
Gunung Pantat Lesong
Sungai Tahan
Kuala Teku Camp
Sungai Peleting
Puteh Camp
S. Puteh
Gunung Rajah 576m (1,890ft)
Sungai Tahan
Sungai Melantai
0 — 5km
0 — 4 miles
Melantai Camp
Sungai Trenggan
Lata Berkoh
S. Tenor
Lubuk Lesong
Sungai Wa
Bumbun Cegar Anjing
Bumbun Tabing
Kuala Trenggan
Park Headquarters
Bukit Teresek
Bumbun Belau
Sungai Tembeling
Bukit Dedari
Kuala Tahan
Taman Negara Resort

ABOVE TOP: AMONGST OVER 300 BIRD
SPECIES IN THE PARK, THE BANDED
PITTA IS A MUCH SOUGHT AFTER PRIZE
FOR ANY BIRDWATCHER.

ABOVE: A VARIETY OF ORCHIDS ADDS A
SPLASH OF COLOUR TO THE DENSE
GREENERY OF THE FOREST.

RIGHT: CYCADS BELONG TO ONE OF
THE WORLD'S MOST ANCIENT GROUPS
OF PLANTS.

LEFT: LOCAL FISHERMEN MAKE A LIVING FROM THE WATERS OF TASIK KENYIR AND OPERATE A BOAT SERVICE INTO THE PARK.

BELOW: TASIK KENYIR WAS CREATED IN 1985 WHEN THE RIVER WAS DAMMED FOR A HYDROELECTRIC SCHEME. TODAY IT OFFERS BOTH A WILDERNESS RETREAT AND AN ALTERNATIVE ACCESS ROUTE INTO THE REMOTE NORTHERN REACHES OF TAMAN NEGARA.

OPPOSITE ABOVE: ALTHOUGH MANY HAVE MOVED TO PERMANENT SETTLE-MENTS OUTSIDE TAMAN NEGARA, A SMALL COMMUNITY OF ORANG ASLI STILL PURSUE A TRADITIONAL HUNTER-GATHERER LIFE INSIDE THE PARK.

OPPOSITE BELOW: THE ENDANGERED STORM'S STORK IS OCCASIONALLY ENCOUNTERED ON THE PARK'S QUIET BACKWATERS.

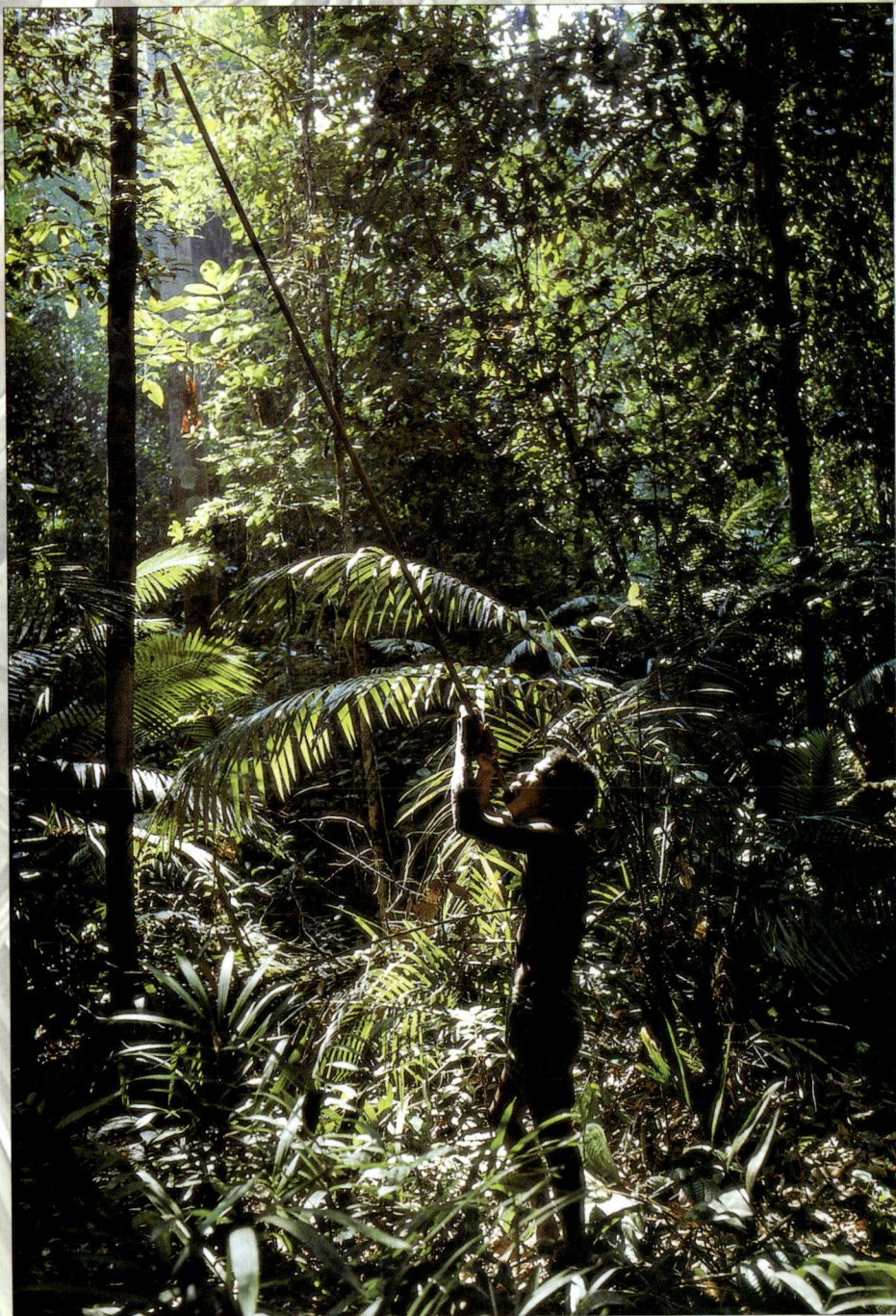

THE ORANG ASLI ARE RENOWNED FOR THEIR HUNTING PROWESS WITH BAMBOO BLOWPIPES.

about 90 minutes out, is a good resting spot and a place to swim.

After leaving the Rentis Tahan to Trenggan trail, the path leads up the headwaters of Sungai Wa and then crosses a fairly steep divide before dropping down to a comfortable campsite at about 200 metres (650 feet) above sea level.

Food dumps for the return journey may be made at this and subsequent camps on the way up. It is best to bury the food in watertight containers or hang it high up out of reach of animals, especially monkeys who are able to get into almost anything.

Sungai Melantai to Kuala Puteh

This is a very tough eight hour leg of the journey that crosses about 25 hills. It involves a series of climbs across an undulating ridge called Bukit Malang (Unlucky Hill) where water is scarce, so it is advisable to fill up before setting off.

Initially, the trail climbs steeply onto a ridge where animal tracks around some of the wallows or wet depressions may be seen. One of the day's last hills, Gunung Rajah at 576 metres (1,890 feet), involves a 150 metre (500 foot) climb that is quite demanding as the day draws to an end.

The last part of the walk is down to Sungai Puteh (White River) and along the river for about 20 minutes before reaching the campsite at its junction with Sungai Tahan. For those who can muster the energy, this is supposedly a good fishing spot.

Kuala Puteh to Kuala Teku

The trail to Kuala Teku requires several river crossings and if water levels are high, an extra four hours may be required to complete this journey, so make an early start. There is plenty of variety in the landscape as the path crosses several sharp spurs and rocky gullies. It then descends to follow Sungai Tahan and crosses the river several times. The trail then climbs high before dropping to the river again just opposite the Kuala Teku campsite. Caution needs to be exercised at the crossings when the water levels are high but if this is the case, guides normally use a different path.

The beautiful campsite at Kuala Teku is located on the other side of the river which must be crossed before the day's journey is completed. For those with some energy remaining at the end of the day, the upper reaches of Sungai Tahan and Sungai Teku are worth exploring.

Kuala Teku to Wray's Camp

This section is the beginning of the real ascent, as the trail climbs from 170 metres (560 feet) altitude to 1,100 metres (3,600 feet) in a steady climb. The day's walk should take about four and a half hours.

Prominent among the large trees along the ridge is the *seraya (Shorea curtisii)* with a red-brown trunk and big buttress roots. The *seraya* tree is indicative of hill dipterocarp forest, as it only occurs in this community and not in the lowland dipterocarp forests. Oak trees, with their characteristic acorn fruits, are present at the higher altitudes. One of Malaysia's six species of conifers also occurs here, *Agathis borneensis*. The tree is identifiable by its mottled dark grey to brown bark which peels off in irregular round flakes. Cones lying on the ground are a sure sign of its presence.

The ridge makes a pronounced turn to the west, and from here on the character of the forest changes dramatically. At this turning is Wray's Camp (also known as Pondok Dua or Second Shelter) named after Leonard Wray, an early explorer and the co-leader of the first botanical survey of Gunung Tahan in 1905.

The site is larger than it looks, with more tent space along a narrow spur running off to the east. From the west side of the camp a trail drops sharply down to the north and a ten minute walk to a small stream where water can always be found.

Walkers who leave Kuala Teku in the morning may find it possible to reach Wray's Camp by lunch time, and then climb on to one of the higher campsites for the evening such as Gunung Pankin on Skeat's Ridge (see below).

Wray's Camp to the Padang.

This day's walk takes about six hours, but there are several good campsites along the way. There is no water on the ridge so it must be carried from Wray's – it is suggested copious amounts be consumed before leaving camp. The climb is difficult throughout this section, very undulating and in some places, near-vertical. The climb across the exposed ridge is arduous work indeed.

Camping is possible in three locations along Skeat's Ridge between Wray's Camp and the Padang. These are Gunung Pankin at 1,463 metres (4,800 feet) above sea level, about one hour walk from Wray's; on the spectacular peak of Gunung Tangga Lima Belas at 1,539 metres (5,050 feet), some two and a half hours from Wray's; or on Gunung Reskit 1,666 metres (5,466 feet), about four hours walk from Wray's at the base of the final climb to the plateau.

The vegetation along the ridge is low with the tallest trees being only about six to seven metres (around 20 feet) in height. The forests are classified as upper montane and along the weathered ridges the trees become dwarfed, gnarled and twisted. Epiphytic lichens such as Old Man's Beard (named because of its long spindly hair-like growth) hang from the branches of the trees. *Leptospermum flavescens* is a common plant found here with its twisted bonsai-like trunk and tiny elliptical leaves (to reduce moisture loss). This is a rather interesting plant and is known as one of the ant trees. At the base of the tree, the *Crematogaster* ant makes its nest in cavities and creates a system of tunnels through the branches and trunk. These ants collect seeds of some epiphytes while removing others.

The conifer, *Dacrydium beccarii* with needle-like leaves is also found in similar areas.

The last part of the climb up to the rim of the plateau basin follows a very steep and difficult gully. The only consolation is that it is sheltered and moist, with tall trees offering protection from the sun.

The top of this gully leads to a small summit called Gunung Tangga Dua Belas. The trails leads on to the southern shoulder of Gunung Gedong at an altitude of 1,830 metres (6,004 feet) above sea level and the plateau is visible from here.

The Padang campsite is about 300 metres (1,000 feet) below this point. The descent takes 30 minutes and if the weather is clear, Gunung Tahan can be seen for the first time on the walk. There is a stream at the campsite.

In the early 1920s a meteorological station was established here, so the weather conditions are well understood. Night temperatures for example, can be as low as 4°C (38°F), so warm sleeping bags are essential. Rain gear is also important as protection from strong winds and rain.

Padang Camp to Gunung Tahan

The plateau is not that large and only covers an area of 15 square kilometres (6 square miles) of open undulating country ranging in altitude from 1,400 to 2,187 metres (4,600 to 7,176 feet). From the Padang campsite the trail continues northwards, alternately crossing streams and spurs until it climbs steeply on to the side of Gunung Gedong, crosses to the ridge linking Gedong with Gunung Tahan, and follows this into a deep saddle. Here, the dense, low forest is rich in ferns, mosses, orchids, and gnarled trees.

The final ascent to the summit is a gentle, steady climb of 350 metres (1,150 feet). In all, the return trip from the campsite takes only about two hours but some extra time should be allocated to look closely at the unique vegetation on the plateau. Caution needs to be exercised as weather changes quickly at this altitude and thick mists can very quickly move in and impede visibility.

At the summit the base rock is sedimentary with some metamorphosed bands of quartzite and pure quartz intrusions. The soil development is poor and mostly infertile and the vegetation that grows here can also be susceptible to drought. Plants are often only a metre (three feet) or so high, but along the streams where peat soils are located, thick stands of shrubs and medium-sized trees are found. The Hill Prinia lives in this habitat, and Gunung Tahan is its only known location in Malaysia. This small brown and white bird has a loud call.

The Gunung Tahan Plateau is a botanically unique area in Peninsular Malaysia. Pitcher plants, orchids, and many other fascinating plants can be found surviving in this location. *Leptospermum flavescens* or *gelam gunung* grows to a height

White-handed Gibbon

of only 3 metres (10 feet) here. The gnarled, dwarfed and twisted trees here are in response to the difficult climatic and soil conditions found on the plateau.

Return Journey

From the Padang campsite the normal return journey reverses the outward route with overnight stops at Kuala Teku and Kuala Puteh, unless an extension is made to the Four Steps Waterfall. (see below)

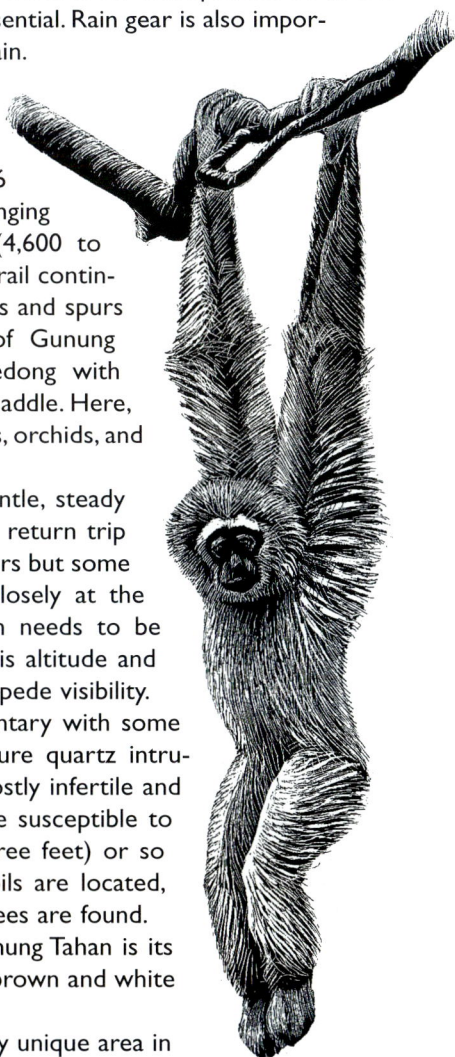

Kuala Teku to Air Terjun Empat Tingkat (Four Steps Waterfall)

On the eastern side of Gunung Tahan and Gunung Gedong the drop into Sungai Tahan is very steep and the waterfall is one of the more spectacular features of the plateau rim. The falls are 50 kilometres (30 miles) walk from Park HQ and normally only attempted by experienced walkers prepared for a few days return journey into the rainforest. The trail starts from the junction of Sungai Teku and Sungai Tahan at Kuala Teku camp site. It follows Sungai Tahan and the waterfall can be reached in one day's walk from Teku Camp.

Those more energetic and adventurous traillists who choose to visit the falls as a side trip from the Gunung Tahan walk, should allocate three day for this additional excursion; two days return walk and one day in which to appreciate the beauty of the falls. The combined Gunung Tahan and Four Steps Waterfall trail then becomes eleven days in total and should only be attempted by serious walkers and those who wish to explore where few others have ventured.

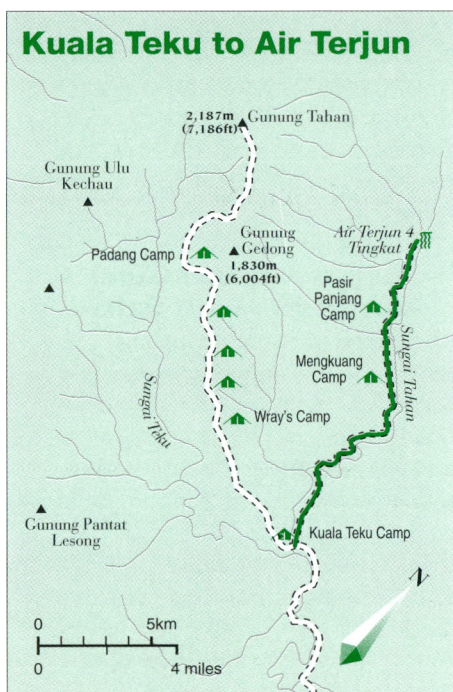

Kuala Teku to Air Terjun

Forbidden Mountain

Gunung Tahan, 'the Forbidden Mountain', has long been the source of local myth and legend. A vast monkey standing guard over two pots of magic stones lives on the summit, according to the folklore of Taman Negara's indigenous people. The Orang Asli people of Taman Negara, the Batek, believe the forest is the home of their ancestors. They hold great respect for their natural environment and only take from it what is necessary for their survival. It is taboo or *lawac* for them to destroy their natural heritage. Originally the Orang Asli had no need to travel and explore the hills because all they needed for survival could be found in the lowland valleys. Today, guides will willingly escort tourist to the summits of Taman Negara's hills and mountains.

The summit of Gunung Tahan defeated the first expedition to attempt to gain it in 1863 when the Sultan of Pahang's team was blocked by the awesome Teku Gorge. Only in 1905 was it finally conquered by a British-Malay expedition led by the explorer Leonard Wray.

7 Other Trails

There are several interesting trails in the less frequented areas of the park, based around the Merapoh and Tasik Kenyir entrances.

7a Sungai Relau to Gunung Tahan via Merapoh, Pahang

The western access to Gunung Tahan is a long way from the main access at Kuala Tahan. This trail is also shorter than the main access at Kuala Tahan, and just five days are recommended (although the return 'run' has been completed in five hours and 38 minutes!). It is affectionately known as the 'West Side Story' by climbers. Getting to the Ranger Station at Sungai Relau is via Merapoh on the Kuala Lipis to Gua Musang road in Pahang State. The turn-off is well signposted and the Ranger Station is just 6 kilometres (4 miles) off the main road (see Entry Formalities).

SUNGAI RELAU TO GUNUNG TAHAN VIA MERAPOH: (7a – 7c)

Start:	Ranger Station Sungai Relau.
Finish:	Ranger Station Sungai Relau.
Duration:	5 days return trip
Distance	Shorter than main route from Kuala Tahan
Best time:	February or March
Conditions:	See Gunung Tahan from Kuala Tahan (Trail 6)
Fitness:	Best for experienced trekkers
Equipment:	See Gunung Tahan from Kuala Tahan (Trail 6)
Regulations:	See Gunung Tahan from Kuala Tahan (Trail 6)

Trail planner

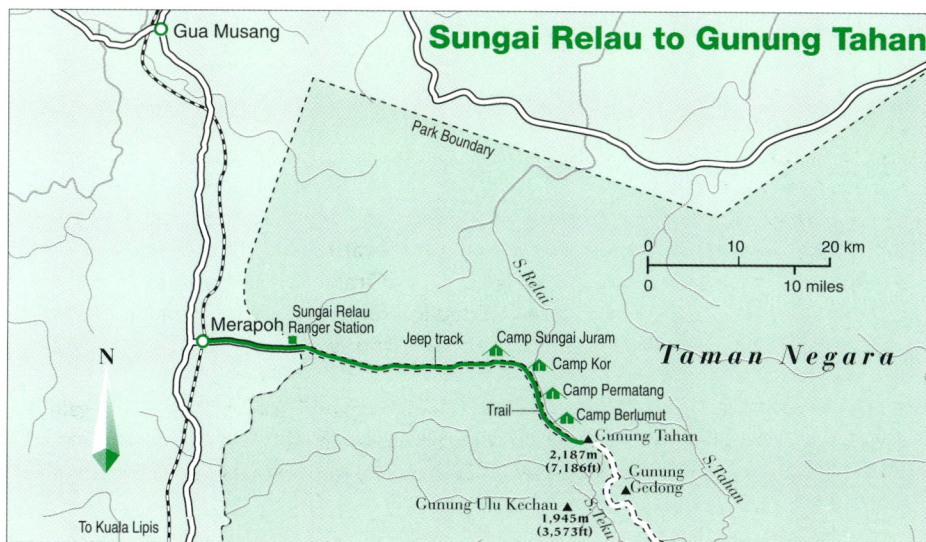

Sungai Relau to Gunung Tahan

- Gua Musang
- Park Boundary
- S. Relau
- Merapoh
- Sungai Relau Ranger Station
- Jeep track
- Camp Sungai Juram
- Camp Kor
- Camp Permatang
- Trail
- Camp Berlumut
- Taman Negara
- Gunung Tahan 2,187m (7,186ft)
- Gunung Gedong
- S. Tahan
- Gunung Ulu Kechau 1,945m (3,573ft)
- S. Tahu
- To Kuala Lipis
- N

0 10 20 km
0 10 miles

Entry fees are paid here and equipment may be left at the Ranger Station for collection on the return journey. There is a camping area besides Sungai Relau and from here – for a fee – most walkers hire the DWNPPM jeep to travel the next 7 kilometres (4½ miles) along a trail to Sungai Juram.

The swing bridge here is the last sign of civilisation for five days. The trail passes through lowland rainforest to the first campsite at Camp Koh besides a river. It involves seven small river crossings and a total hiking time of about four hours.

The trail starts to climb gently on Day 2 until near vertical sections are reached near Gunung Tahan. Faster walkers can reduce the nights spent on this trek by camping on the summit. But staying on the summit overnight means that groups have to be properly equipped for a cold night.

7b Kuala Koh: Fig Tree Trail

Most points of access in this part of the park are via rivers, however, there is a nice short, labelled walk called the Fig Tree Trail (Bulatan Ara). Informative track notes are available from the Ranger Station. The interpretation trail was developed by MNS, DANCED and Perhilitan and takes about two hours depending on interest and stops en route.

The trail is hilly and should only be attempted by those who are fit. It commences across the river, opposite the Ranger Station, at the suspension bridge. Points of interest are numbered and visitors are advised to look at the interpretation display in the Ranger Station first to get a good understanding of the rainforest ecosystem.

The trail passes bamboo, epiphytes, ferns, lianas, buttress roots, ginger flowers, rattan, strangler figs, wild hibiscus, fungi and the fig tree. The trail is a very good introduction to the rainforest, as it exhibits most of the features of this ecosystem.

Listen for the White-rumped Shama in the forest as well as signs of other animals, like Wild Boar diggings along the trails.

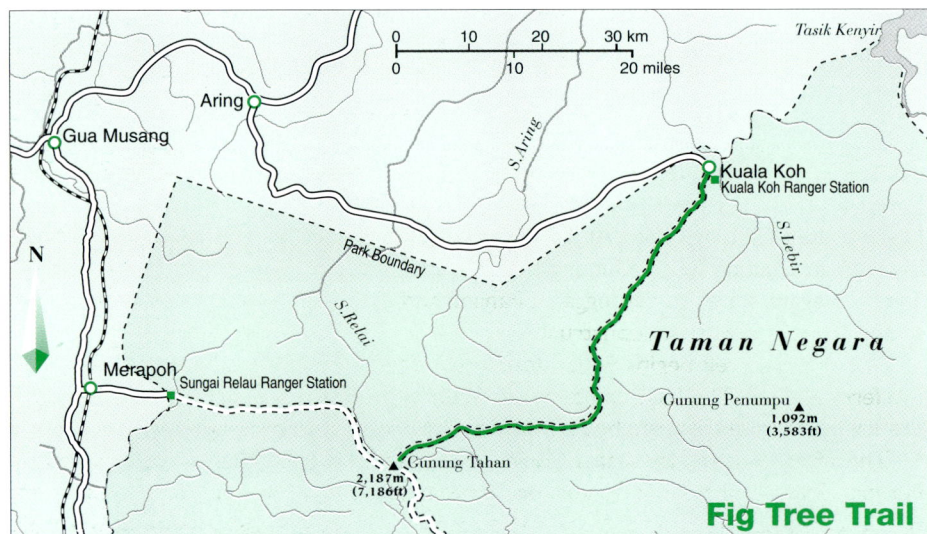

Fig Tree Trail

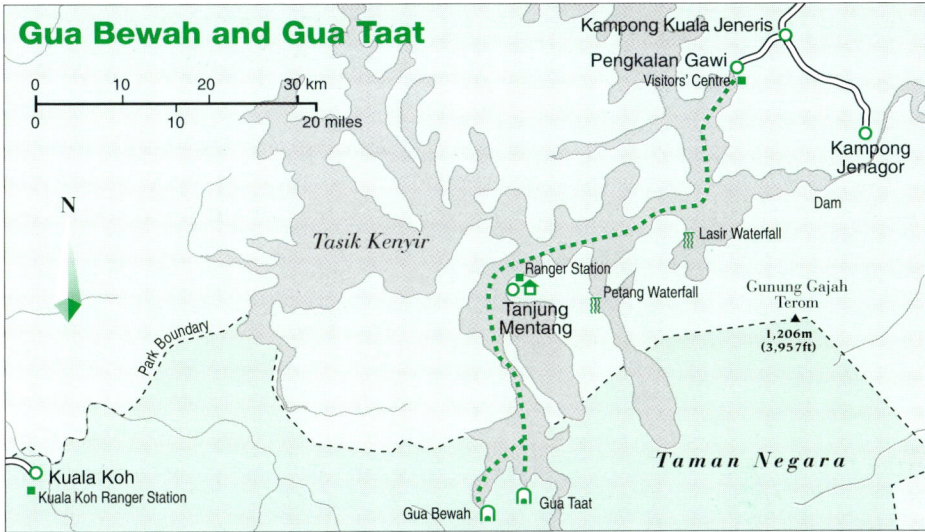

Gua Bewah and Gua Taat

Kampong Kuala Jeneris
Pengkalan Gawi
Visitors' Centre
Kampong Jenagor
Dam
Lasir Waterfall
Ranger Station
Petang Waterfall
Gunung Gajah Terom
Tanjung Mentang
1,206m (3,957ft)
Tasik Kenyir
N
Park Boundary
Taman Negara
Kuala Koh
Kuala Koh Ranger Station
Gua Bewah
Gua Taat

7c Terengganu: Gua Bewah and Gua Taat

The caves are located within some towering limestone mountains on the foreshores of Tasik Kenyir. To reach the caves takes one and a half to two hours fast boat journey from the Visitors' Centre at Pengkalan Gawi.

From across the lake the vertical rise from the water's edge is a photogenic sight. The walk to the caves is not so much a trail as a ten minute climb up some well constructed wooden steps. One of the entrances is submerged under the lake's waters, however it is possible to enter the other two caves if the dam water level is not too high. One entrance is close to the lake's edge. The stalactites and stalagmites deep within the caves are reasonably well developed but a torch is essential to see them properly. The cave entrance is large and the high view across the lake is quite impressive. The caves have historical significance in that archaeological digs have uncovered artefacts and tools dating back to the Neolithic Period, about 6,000 years ago.

7d Gunung Gagau Trail

Just beyond Tasik Kenyir stands Gunung Gagua, the second highest peak in Taman Negara after Gunung Tahan. At 1,377 metres (4,518 feet) it is however, substantially lower than Gunung Tahan. Gunung Gagua is located right on the border of the three Taman Negara states of Terengganu, Pahang and Kelantan. A base campsite and trails to the summit have been constructed.

This five day trek begins with a four hour slow boat trip across Tasik Kenyir from the ferry at Gawi. The base camp can sometimes be difficult to reach, depending upon the level of the lake. Faster boats make the journey in under two hours

The afternoon of day one involves a five hour trek to the campsite at Sungai Perepet. This is followed the next day by a morning walk to Sungai Cicir camp and then an arduous five hour climb to the summit of Gunung Gagau. The next two nights

119

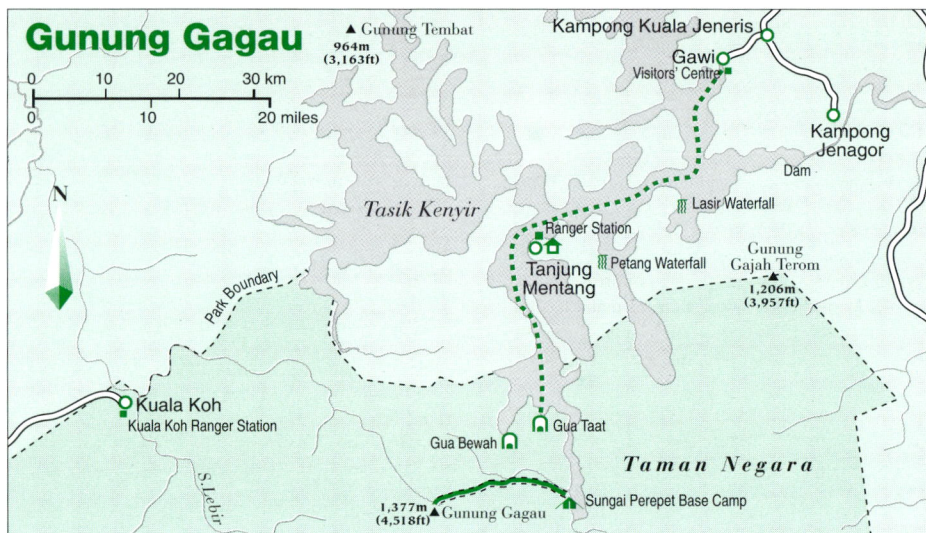

Gunung Gagau

Gunung Tembat 964m (3,163ft)

Kampong Kuala Jeneris

Gawi
Visitors' Centre

Kampong Jenagor

Dam

Lasir Waterfall

Tasik Kenyir

Ranger Station

Tanjung Mentang

Petang Waterfall

Gunung Gajah Terom 1,206m (3,957ft)

Park Boundary

N

Kuala Koh
Kuala Koh Ranger Station

S. Lebir

Gua Bewah

Gua Taat

Taman Negara

1,377m (4,518ft) Gunung Gagau

Sungai Perepet Base Camp

are spent camping at Gunung Gagau. Day three entails a return walk to Gunung Badong and back to the Day 2 campsite.

The return journey to Sungai Perpek makes for a relatively short fourth day, and the return boat is usually arranged for the following morning. The climb to the summit tends to be long and gentle with the steepest sections between Sungai Cicir Camp and the summit. The fishing around the Base Camp at Sungai Perpek is good but a license is required.

Trekkers need to ensure that adequate arrangements are made to be collected at the end of the trek — it is a long way to swim back to Pengkalan Gawi.

GUNUNG GAGAU (7d)

Start:	Pengkalan Gawi Visitors' Centre
Finish:	Pengkalan Gawi Visitors' Centre
Distance:	30 km (19 miles) return (excluding boat journey)
Duration:	5 days round trip
Best time:	February or March
Conditions:	Lower altitudes: rainforest and rivers. Higher altitudes: mountain ridges and gullies.
Fitness:	Best for experienced trekkers
Equipment:	Light clothing for day; warm clothes for mountain nights (no shelter). Trekking boots and raincape. Camping and cooking gear, food and water. Torch and batteries. Leech socks and insect repellent. Binoculars and camera.
Regulations:	Guide compulsory. Fishing licence required.

Trail planner

Address Book

TOUR OPERATORS

Several tour operators bring people to the park and some operate just within the park. When making bookings by telephone, remember the international dialling prefix for Malaysia is '60'. When calling from outside the country delete the first '0' from the local code, e.g. to dial a Kuala Lumpur number from within Malaysia the code is '03', from outside Malaysia dial '603'.

NATIONAL OPERATORS

Asian Overland Services (AOS)
39C & 40C Jalan Mamanda 9
Ampang Point
Ampang
68000 Kuala Lumpur
Tel: 03 42591000, Fax: 03 42529800, e mail: aos@aostt.po.my
AOS is the largest inbound operator in Malaysia and has been conducting tours for a long time. They have offices and affiliates throughout the country as well as their own guides in the park.

Impressions Holidays and Resorts
33 Jalan 2/76C
Desa Pandan
55100 Kuala Lumpur
Tel: 03 2411096, Fax: 03 2019698
This company arranges bus transfers to and from Kuala Tembeling, the riverfront departure point for Taman Negara. The normal collection point in Kuala Lumpur is the Istana Hotel.

Kingfisher Tours
Suite 1107, 11th Floor
Bangunan Yayasan Selangor
Jalan Bukit Bintang
55100 Kuala Lumpur
P.O. Box 50766
Kuala Lumpur
Tel: 03 2421454
Fax: 03 2429827
This well established wildlife tour company specialises in tailor-made tours for small, special interest groups

Trans Titiwangsa Explorer
Lot 8B, Level 2,
Jalan Pejabat Pos
Sungei Besi
57100 Kuala Lumpur
Tel/Fax: 03 94588242

LOCAL OPERATORS

Ismail Travel & Tours
Taman Negara
Kuala Tahan
27000 Jerantut
Te: 09 2669744/2667855
Specialists in budget tours, transportation, accommodation, guide services and fishing trips.

Safarin Adventure Expedition
Taman Negara
Kuala Tahan
27000 Jerantut
Tel: 09 2661122, Fax: 09 2661500, mobile: 010 9883508
Safarin Mohd. Yassim is an experienced guide and can arrange water rafting, canoeing, fishing, camping, Gunung Tahan expeditions and night walks.

S I Travel & Tours
Lot 2, Jalan Sultan Mahmud
20400 Kuala Terengganu
Te : 09 6237000, Fax: 09 6231144
Specialist operators who provide a range of tours to Tasik Kenyir, fishing expeditions and camping at the lake, and the Terengganu side of Taman Negara.

Taman Negara Resort (TNR)
Kuala Tahan
27000 Jerantut
Pahang
Tel: 09 2662200, Fax: 09 2663500
Bookings can be made through a Kuala Lumpur sales office (Tel: 245 5585, Fax: 245 5430, e mail: taman_negararst@hotmail.com) or direct to the resort. Most visitors to Taman Negara stay in the TNR. It is the preferred accommodation for package tours and tour operators. They also organise guides and tours within the park, and all enquiries should be directed to the front desk at the resort. Website: http://www@tradestar.com/negara

CONSERVATION ORGANISATIONS AND DEPARTMENTS

Association of Backpackers Malaysia
6 Jalan SS3/33
47300 Petaling Jaya
Tel/Fax: 03 78756249
The association is one of Malaysia's best known and respected outdoor groups. They conduct regular walks and expeditions to various parts of the country including all parts of Taman Negara.

Department of Wildlife and National Parks of Peninsular Malaysia (Perhilitan) DWNPPM

Kuala Lumpur Office
Kilometre 10, Jalan Cheras
56100, Kuala Lumpur.
Tel: 03 90752872, Fax:03 90752873
e mail: kp@jphltn.sains.my
website: http://www.jaring.my/hilitan/

Gua Musang Office (for Kuala Koh)
Tel/Fax: 09 9122940

Kuala Tahan Office
Taman Negara
Kuala Tahan
27000 Jerantut
Tel: 09 2661122, Fax: 09 2664110

Merapoh Office
Sungai Relau
Merapoh
Tel/Fax: 09 9124894

Terengganu Office
4th Floor
Wisma Persekutuan
20200 Kuala Terengganu
Terengganu
Tel: 09 6221460, Fax: 09 6241326

Forest Research Institute Malaysia (FRIM)
Kepong
52109 Kuala Lumpur
Tel: 03 62742633, Fax: 03 62767753
The leading forest research institute in Malaysia and the best place to talk to those who know the forests well. For visitors with a real interest in rainforest ecology this is also a good place to visit. There are signposted nature trails, an arboretum, canopy walk, Environmental Education Centre and a museum. There is a regular bus service to FRIM.

Malaysian Nature Society (MNS)
JKR 641
Jalan Kelantan
Bukit Persekutuan
50480 Kuala Lumpur
P.O. Box 10750
50724 Kuala Lumpur
Tel: 03 32892294, Fax: 03 32894311
e mail: natsoc@po.jaring.my
website: http//www.mns.org.my/mns
One of Malaysia's leading environmental NGOs that conducts research and educational activities, produces reports and publications on Malaysia's environment, and conducts field trips for members and the general public. They also have special interest groups who conduct outdoor activities throughout the country.

Wetlands International
3A, 37 Kelana Centre Point
Kelana Jaya
No 3 Jalan SS7/19
47300 Petaling Jaya
Tel: 03 7046770, Fax: 03 7046772
e mail: wiap@wiap.nasionet.net
website: http://ngo.asiapac.net/wetlands
An international authority on wetlands and associated ecosystems. The Kuala Lumpur office is engaged in environmental consultancy, education and policy planning for wetland areas in Asia and the Pacific.

World Wide Fund For Nature (WWF) Malaysia or Tabung Alam Malaysia
49 Jalan SS23/15
Taman SEA
Petaling Jaya 47400
Tel : 7033772, Fax : 7035157
e mail: wwfmal@wwfnet.org
website: http://www.wwfmal.cjb.net
WWF Malaysia, established as a charity in 1972, is one of Malaysia's leading conservation organisations. Its work encompasses scientific field research, policy advocacy and fund raising activities, as well as environmental education and awareness programmes. It also works closely with other NGOs and government agencies to carry out conservation projects nationwide. WWF Malaysia has produced numerous publications and resources for educational and awareness purposes. For more information contact the office in Petalang Jaya or log on to its website.

Tourism Malaysia Offices

Malaysia Tourism Promotion Board
17th Floor, 24-27th & 30th Floors
Menara Dato' Onn
Putra World Trade Centre
45 Jalan Tun Ismail
50480 Kuala Lumpur
Tel : 26935188, Fax: 03 26935884
e mail: tourism@tourism.gov.my
website: http://tourism.gov.my
MTPB operates a General Tourist Information Counter on the Ground Floor of this building from 0900 –1800, daily. Enquiries can be directed to Tel : 26936664 or 21643929.
Internationally they operate offices in: Sydney (Tel: 02 92994441), Singapore (Tel: 02 5326321), South Africa (Tel: 011 3270400), United Kingdom (Tel: 0171 9307932) and the United States (Tel: 212 7541113).

Further Reading

Bransbury, J. 1993. *A Birdwatcher's Guide to Malaysia.* Waymark Publishing. This book is an excellent guide to the birdwatching sites in Malaysia.

Davison, G. and G. Cubitt. 1999. *The National Parks and Other Wild Places of Malaysia.* New Holland Publishers, London. Large format, pictorial reference book to the many natural attractions of Malaysia. There is a chapter dedicated to Taman Negara.

Davison, G.W.H. and Chew Yen Fook, 1995. *A Photographic Guide to the Birds of Peninsular Malaysia and Singapore.* New Holland Publishers, London. A small, lightweight but informative photographic guide to many of the species found in Taman Negara.

Department of Wildlife and National Parks. Undated. *Taman Negara Malaysia.* Government Printer, Kuala Lumpur. Unfortunately this booklet is not widely available and probably confined to libraries and department archives. It has detailed background information on the many sites within the park and trail notes for wildlife enthusiasts.

Jeyarajasincham A. and Pearson A, 1999. *A Fieldguide to the Birds of West Malaysia and Singapore.* Oxford University Press. An up to date guide to the birds of Peninsular Malaysia and Singapore.

Malaysian Timber Council, 1998. *Malaysia's Green Attractions: A Guide to Discovering Malaysia's Natural Areas, Parks, Trees, Plants and Animals.* Falcon Press, Kuala Lumpur. There are two booklets in this package; one contains a colourful and general introduction to the many natural attractions of Malaysia while the other answers the essential questions for visitors to specific sites. There are entries for both the Kuala Tahan and Kuala Koh entry points to Taman Negara. This is a very useful introduction for visitors who intend to visit several of Malaysia's natural attractions. Available in major bookshops or by contacting the Malaysian Timber Council in Kuala Lumpur on Tel: 03 9811999 or London Tel: 171 2228188. Home Page: http://www.mtc.com.my e mail: ceo@mtc.com.my.

Moore, W (Ed.), 1990. *Heritage Mapbook of Peninsular Malaysia.* Falcon Press, Kuala Lumpur. A very useful map guide to the whole of Peninsular Malaysia with specific reference to attractions along the various routes to the National Park. This user-friendly guide provides details of accommodation, speciality restaurants, charges (although these should be used as a guide only) and brief details on history and things to see. It is well illustrated with many coloured photographs and detailed maps. E mail: falcon@po.jaring.my.

Payne, J and G. Cubitt. 1990. *Wild Malaysia.* New Holland Publishers, London. Excellent pictorial reference to the main natural attractions in Malaysia.

Robson, C. 2000. *Field Guide to the Birds of South-East Asia.* New Holland Publishers, London. The most recent field guide with full descriptions and illustrations of the 1,250 bird species found in the region.

Sham Sani (edit), 1998. *The Encyclopaedia of Malaysia: The Environment.* Editions Didier Millet, Kuala Lumpur. A detailed description of Malaysia's environment and threats to it with contributions from the country's leading authorities.

Soepadmo, E. (edit), 1998. *The Encyclopaedia of Malaysia: Plants.* Editions Didier Millet, Kuala Lumpur. Very detailed description of the plants found in Malaysia with contributions from the country's leading botanists and biologists.

Strange, M. 1998 *Birds of South-East Asia: A Photographic Guide.* New Holland Publishers, London. Well-documented and photographic guide to over 250 birds from 40 families. Gives advice on how to locate and identify the birds.

Tweedie, M.W.F. 1978. *Mammals of Malaysia.* Longman Malaysia. An informative introduction with good colour plates of the more significant species.

Yong Hoi Sen (edit), 1998. *The Encyclopaedia of Malaysia: Animals.* Editions Didier Millet, Kuala Lumpur. Part of a series on Malaysia, packed with information, facts, excellent photographs and descriptive diagrams.

Checklist of birds of Taman Negara

- ❑ Storm's Stork
- ❑ Little Heron
- ❑ Black Bittern
- ❑ Bat Hawk
- ❑ Crested Honey-buzzard
- ❑ Crested Goshawk
- ❑ Blyth's Hawk-eagle
- ❑ Wallace's Hawk-eagle
- ❑ Changeable Hawk-eagle
- ❑ Black Eagle
- ❑ Lesser Fish-eagle
- ❑ Crested Serpent-eagle\
- ❑ Osprey
- ❑ Black-thighed Falconet
- ❑ Peregrine Falcon
- ❑ Long-billed Partridge
- ❑ Scaly-breasted Partridge
- ❑ Crested Wood-partridge
- ❑ Crestless Fireback
- ❑ Crested Fireback
- ❑ Red Junglefowl
- ❑ Malaysian Peacock-pheasant
- ❑ Mountain Peacock-pheasant
- ❑ Crested Argus
- ❑ Great Argus
- ❑ Common Sandpiper
- ❑ Wedge-tailed Pigeon
- ❑ Large Green Pigeon
- ❑ Little Green Pigeon
- ❑ Pink-necked Pigeon
- ❑ Jambu Fruit Pigeon
- ❑ Green Imperial Pigeon
- ❑ Mountain Imperial Pigeon
- ❑ Little Cuckoo-dove
- ❑ Spotted Dove
- ❑ Emerald Dove
- ❑ Long-tailed Parakeet
- ❑ Blue-rumped Parrot
- ❑ Blue-crowned Hanging-parrot
- ❑ Large Hawk-cuckoo
- ❑ Hodgson's Hawk-cuckoo
- ❑ Indian Cuckoo
- ❑ Plaintive Cuckoo
- ❑ Malayan Bronze Cuckoo
- ❑ Drongo Cuckoo
- ❑ Black-bellied Malkoha

- ❑ Chestnut-bellied Malkoha
- ❑ Green-billed Malkoha
- ❑ Raffles's Malkoha
- ❑ Chestnut-breasted Malkoha
- ❑ Red-billed Malkoha
- ❑ Short-toed Coucal
- ❑ Greater Coucal
- ❑ Mountain Scops-owl
- ❑ Collared Scops-owl
- ❑ Reddish Scops-owl
- ❑ Barred Eagle Owl
- ❑ Collared Owlet
- ❑ Brown Hawk Owl
- ❑ Gould's Frogmouth
- ❑ Malaysian Eared Nightjar
- ❑ Grey Nightjar
- ❑ Large-tailed Nightjar
- ❑ White-bellied Swiftlet
- ❑ Silver-rumped Swift
- ❑ Fork-tailed Swift
- ❑ Asian Palm Swift
- ❑ Grey-rumped Tree-swift
- ❑ Whiskered Tree-swift
- ❑ Red-naped Trogon
- ❑ Diard's Trogon
- ❑ Orange-breasted Trogon
- ❑ Common Kingfisher
- ❑ Blue-eared Kingfisher
- ❑ Blue-banded Kingfisher
- ❑ Black-backed Kingfisher
- ❑ Rufous-backed Kingfisher
- ❑ Stork-billed Kingfisher
- ❑ White-throated Kingfisher
- ❑ Black-capped Kingfisher
- ❑ Collared Kingfisher
- ❑ Chestnut-headed Bee-eater
- ❑ Blue-throated Bee-eater
- ❑ Blue-tailed Bee-eater
- ❑ Red-bearded Bee-eater
- ❑ Dollarbird
- ❑ White-crowned Hornbill
- ❑ Bushy-crested Hornbill
- ❑ Wreathed Hornbill
- ❑ Wrinkled Hornbill
- ❑ Pied Hornbill
- ❑ Black Hornbill
- ❑ Great Hornbill

- ❑ Rhinoceros Hornbill
- ❑ Helmeted Hornbill
- ❑ Gold-whiskered Barbet
- ❑ Red-throated Barbet
- ❑ Golden-throated Barbet
- ❑ Black-browed Barbet
- ❑ Yellow-crowned Barbet
- ❑ Blue-eared Barbet
- ❑ Brown Barbet
- ❑ Rufous Piculet
- ❑ Rufous Woodpecker
- ❑ Grey-headed Woodpecker
- ❑ Crimson-winged Woodpecker
- ❑ Lesser Yellownape
- ❑ Checker-throated Woodpecker
- ❑ Banded Woodpecker
- ❑ Common Flameback
- ❑ Olive-backed Woodpecker
- ❑ Buff-rumped Woodpecker
- ❑ Buff-necked Woodpecker
- ❑ Great Slaty Woodpecker
- ❑ White-bellied Woodpecker
- ❑ Grey-capped Woodpecker
- ❑ Grey-and-Buff Woodpecker
- ❑ Orange-backed Woodpecker
- ❑ Green Broadbill
- ❑ Black-and-Yellow Broadbill
- ❑ Banded Broadbill
- ❑ Black-and-Red Broadbill
- ❑ Dusky Broadbill
- ❑ Long-tailed Broadbill
- ❑ Giant Pitta
- ❑ Garnet Pitta
- ❑ Banded Pitta
- ❑ Hooded Pitta
- ❑ Blue-winged Pitta
- ❑ Barn Swallow
- ❑ Pacific Swallow
- ❑ Red-rumped Swallow
- ❑ Large Wood-shrike
- ❑ Large Cuckoo-shrike
- ❑ Bar-bellied Cuckoo-shrike
- ❑ Lesser Cuckoo-shrike
- ❑ Bar-winged Flycatcher-shrike

- Black-winged Flycatcher-shrike
- Grey-chinned Minivet
- Scarlet Minivet
- Ashy Minivet
- Puff-backed Bulbul
- Black-and-White Bulbul
- Black-headed Bulbul
- Scaly-breasted Bulbul
- Grey-bellied Bulbul
- Straw-headed Bulbul
- Stripe-throated Bulbul
- Yellow-vented Bulbul
- Olive-winged Bulbul
- Spectacled Bulbul
- Cream-vented Bulbul
- Red-eyed Bulbul
- Grey-cheeked Bulbul
- Yellow-bellied Bulbul
- Ochraceous Bulbul
- Finsch's Bulbul
- Hairy-backed Bulbul
- Buff-vented Bulbul
- Olive Bulbul
- Ashy Bulbul
- Green Iora
- Common Iora
- Lesser Green Leafbird
- Greater Green Leafbird
- Blue-winged Leafbird
- Asian Fairy Bluebird
- Crow-billed Drongo
- Bronzed Drongo
- Lesser Racket-tailed Drongo
- Greater Racket-tailed Drongo
- Dark-throated Oriole
- Crested Jay
- Common Green Magpie
- Black Magpie
- Slender-billed Crow
- Velvet-fronted Nuthatch
- Blue Nuthatch
- White-throated Fantail
- Spotted Fantail
- Grey-headed Flycatcher
- Verditer Flycatcher
- Asian Brown Flycatcher
- Ferruginous Flycatcher
- Pygmy Blue Flycatcher
- White-tailed Flycatcher
- Pale Blue Flycatcher
- Malaysian Blue Flycatcher
- Hill Blue Flycatcher
- Rufous-chested Flycatcher
- Little Pied Flycatcher
- Rufous-browed Flycatcher
- Grey-chested Jungle Flycatcher
- Rufous-winged Philentoma
- Maroon-breasted Philentoma
- Black-naped Blue Monarch
- Asian Paradise Flycatcher
- Japanese Paradise Flycatcher
- Malaysian Rail Babbler
- Black-capped Babbler
- Short-tailed Babbler
- White-chested Babbler
- Ferruginous Babbler
- Horsfield's Babbler
- Abbott's Babbler
- Rufous-crowned Babbler
- Scaly-crowned Babbler
- Moustached Babbler
- Sooty-capped Babbler
- Grey-breasted Babbler
- Chestnut-backed Scimitar-babbler
- Large Scimitar-babbler
- Striped Wren-babbler
- Streaked Wren-babbler
- Eyebrowed Wren-babbler
- Pygmy Wren-babbler
- Striped Tit-babbler
- Fluffy-backed Tit-babbler
- Grey-throated Babbler
- Grey-headed Babbler
- Black-throated Babbler
- Chestnut-rumped Babbler
- Chestnut-winged Babbler
- Rufous-fronted Babbler
- Golden Babbler
- Silver-eared Mesia
- White-browed Shrike-babbler
- Black-eared Shrike-babbler
- Rufous-winged Fulvetta
- Mountain Fulvetta
- Brown Fulvetta
- Chestnut-tailed Minla
- Blue-winged Minla
- White-bellied Yuhina
- Long-tailed Sibia
- Golden-bellied Gerygone
- Hill Prinia
- Mountain Leaf-warbler
- Arctic Warbler
- Eastern Crowned Warbler
- Chestnut-crowned Warbler
- Mountain Tailorbird
- Dark-necked Tailorbird
- Common Tailorbird
- Rufous-tailed Tailorbird
- Siberian Blue Robin
- Lesser Shortwing
- Rufous-tailed Shama
- Oriental Magpie Robin
- White-rumped Shama
- White-crowned Forktail
- Chestnut-naped Forktail
- Slaty-backed Forktail
- Eyebrowed Thrush
- Grey Wagtail
- Tiger Shrike
- Yellow-breasted Flowerpecker
- Crimson-breasted Flowerpecker
- Yellow-vented Flowerpecker
- Buff-bellied Flowerpecker
- Orange-bellied Flowerpecker
- Brown-throated Sunbird
- Red-throated Sunbird
- Ruby-cheeked Sunbird
- Purple-naped Sunbird
- Black-throated Sunbird
- Little Spiderhunter
- Long-billed Spiderhunter
- Spectacled Spiderhunter
- Grey-breasted Spiderhunter
- Everett's White-eye
- Philippine Glossy Starling
- Common Myna
- Hill Myna
- Eurasian Tree-sparrow
- Brown Bullfinch

Glossary

Abiotic: non-living matter.

Angiosperm: Flowering plant.

Bacteria: smallest living organisms; with fungi, they comprise the decomposer level of the food-chain.

Biodegradable: capable of being broken down by bacteria or other natural means.

Biodiversity: number and variety of both plant and animal species.

Biotic: living matter.

Bryophytes: plant division that includes mosses, hornworts, and liverworts.

Carpel: female reproductive organ of a flowering plant.

Carnivore: meat-eating organism.

Catchment area: area drained by a single river.

Deciduous: (of trees) shedding leaves seasonally.

Decomposer: organism, such as a fungus or bacterium, that breaks down dead matter.

Deforestation: the clearing of trees on a large scale.

Diurnal: predominantly active during daylight hours.

Dipterocarp: tree belonging to the family Dipterocarpaceae, the main source of Malaysian hardwood timber.

Ecology: branch of science that deals with the inter-relationship between organisms and their environment.

Ecosystem: interdependence of species in the living world with one another and their environment. Ecosystems encompass communities of all sizes, from a pond, through a rainforest to a continent.

Effluent: waste substance, particularly a liquid, that enters the environment from a point source.

Endemic: native plant or animal of a specific, localised area.

Epiphyte: plant that uses other plants, often trees, for support but without drawing nutrients from its host.

Evergreen: tree or shrub that never sheds all its leaves completely.

Fauna: all the animal life of a given place or time.

Flora: all the plant life of a given place or time.

Food chain: a sequence of organisms, each of which feeds on other organisms lower down the chain.

Food web: complex, interlocking series of food chains.

Forest canopy: uppermost layer of a forest.

Fungus: non-photosynthetic organisms that obtain nutrients by absorbing organic compounds from their surroundings.

Herbivore: plant-eating organism..

Humus: a mass of partially decomposed organic matter in the soil that improves its fertility and ability to retain water.

Indigenous: native to a particular place.

Insecticide: substance or mixture of substances intended to prevent, destroy or repel insects.

Laterite: iron rich soil found in some tropical areas.

Leaching: extraction or flushing out of dissolved or suspended materials from soil by high rainfall.

Liana: vine-like, woody, free-climbing plants that are a characteristic of rainforests.

Lichen: a composite organism comprising a fungus and an alga in a symbiotic relationship.

Metamorphic: something that has changed its physical state – in most cases this refers to rocks that have been altered by intense heat and pressure.

Micro-organism: generally, any living thing of microscopic size, including bacteria, yeasts, simple fungi, some algae, slime moulds and protozoans.

Monoculture: cultivation of a single crop (such as rubber or oil palm) to the exclusion of other plants.

Monsoon: the seasonal variation in tropical winds that results in distinct wet and dry seasons.

Nocturnal: predominantly more active at night.

Nutrient: elements or compounds that are essential raw materials for the growth of organisms.

Omnivore: animals such as humans that consume both plants and animals for food.

Organism: any living individual plant or animal.

Parasite: plant that lives on, or in, another host plant from which it obtains water, nutrients and shelter.

Pesticide: any chemical designed to kill fungi, weeds, insects, pests and other organisms that humans considerto be undesirable.

Photosynthesis: biological process by which plants make food energy through the use of sunlight, water and carbon dioxide.

Predator: organism that lives by killing and eating other organisms.

Prophylaxis: preventative medicine, for example against malaria.

Recycle: the re-use of a resource, e.g. glass bottles being melted down to make new glass.

Saprophyte: plant that absorbs organic nutrients from inanimate sources such as dung or dead wood. Fungi are the most common form of saprophytes.

Species: a single kind of organism that breeds only with its own kind.

Strangling fig: a type of fig tree that germinates in the crown of the host tree, sending roots downwards where they link up and envelop the host tree, eventually killing it.

Subsidence: sinking down of part of the Earth's crust.

Sustainable: capable of being maintained at a steady pace without exhausting natural resources or causing severe environmental damage over time (for example, sustainable development).

Transpiration: direct transfer of water from the leaves of living plants into the atmosphere.

Topography: the surface configuration of the land.

Vascular Plants: those that obtain moisture and nutrients from the soil.

Watershed: the land area from which water drains toward a common water course in a natural basin.

Weathering: the process of rock and mineral disintegration at the Earth's surface.

Wilderness: a natural area mostly undisturbed by humans and where humans themselves are temporary visitors.

Index

Page numbers in **bold** refer to illustrations.